ARTISTIC ADVENTURES

ART DECO MAGIC :

A COLORING BOOK FOR ADULTS

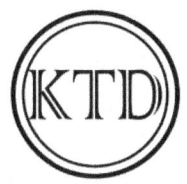 **KATE TAYLOR DESIGN**

This book features 40 intricate illustrations. Each illustration is printed on one side of the page, providing a convenient and enjoyable coloring experience for adults.

SCAN ME

If you would like to reorder, please scan the QR Code

ART DECO

is a style of visual arts and design that emerged in the 1920s and 1930s. It is characterized by bold geometric shapes, stylized forms, and ornate details. Art Deco drew inspiration from a variety of sources, including ancient cultures, modern industrialization, and the machine age. It was a popular style for architecture, fashion, and art, and was associated with luxury, glamour, and modernity. Today, Art Deco remains an influential and distinctive style that is celebrated for its striking aesthetic and historical significance.

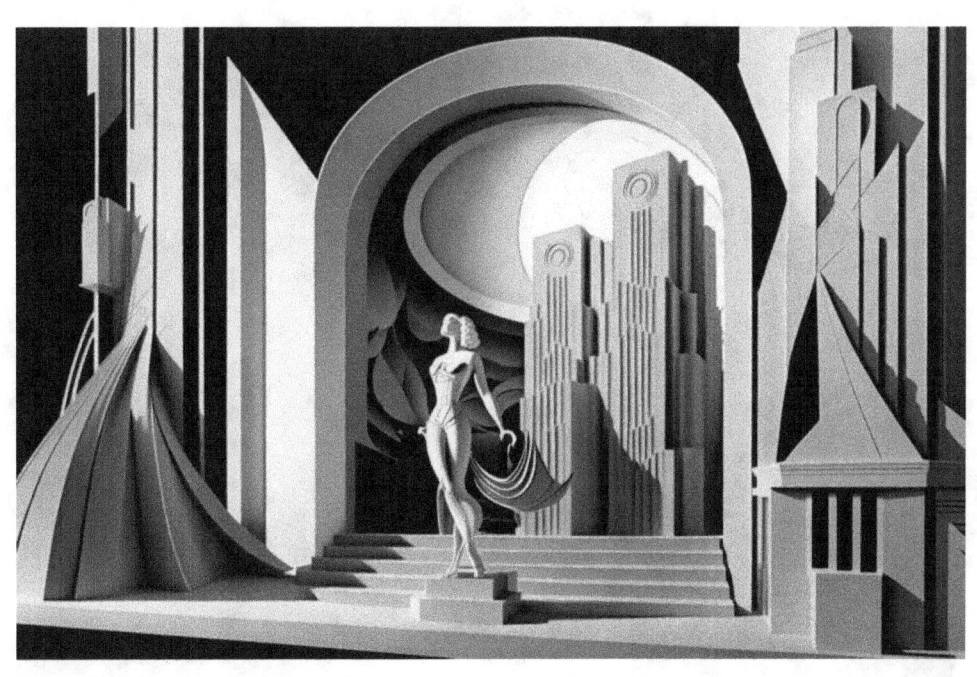

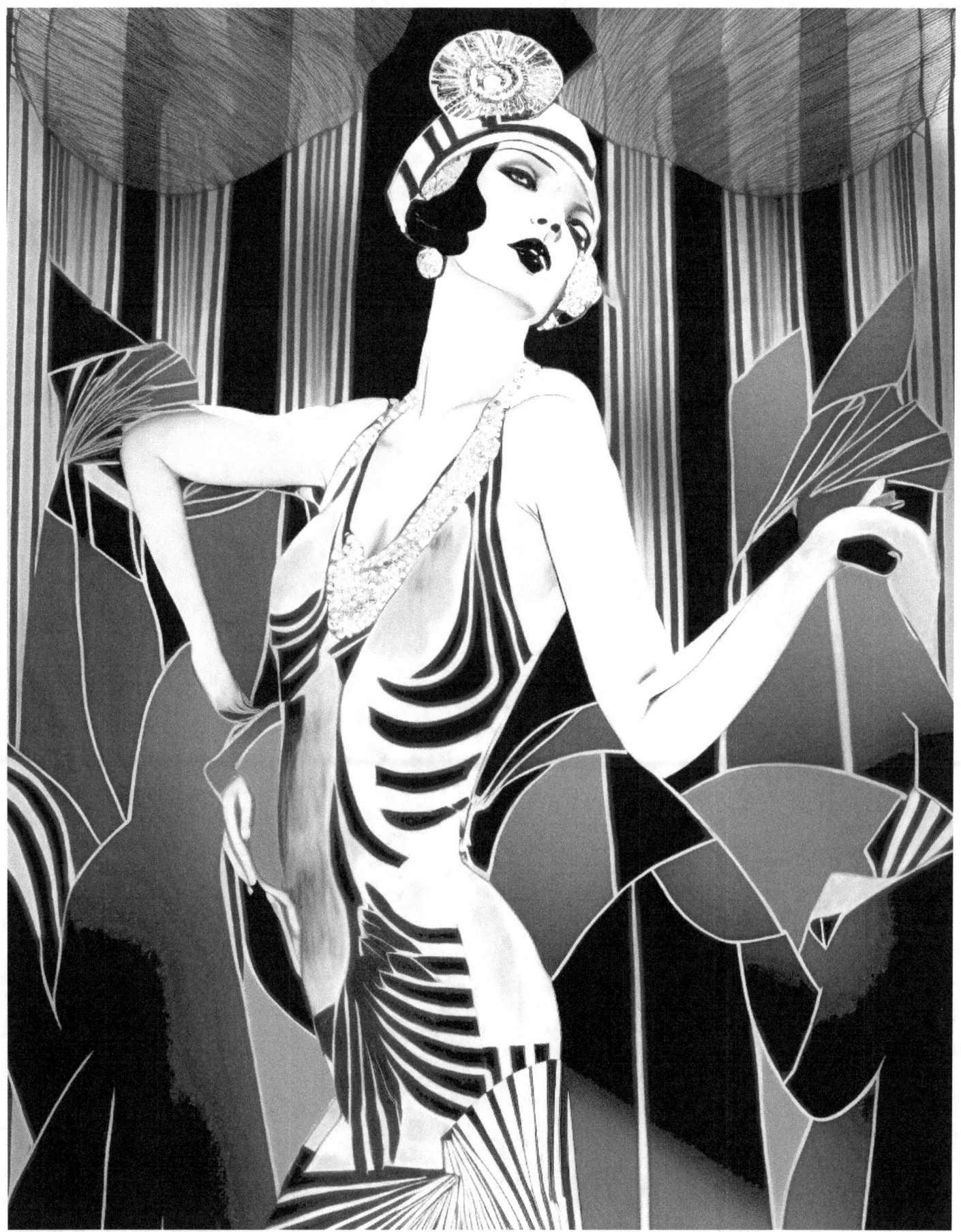

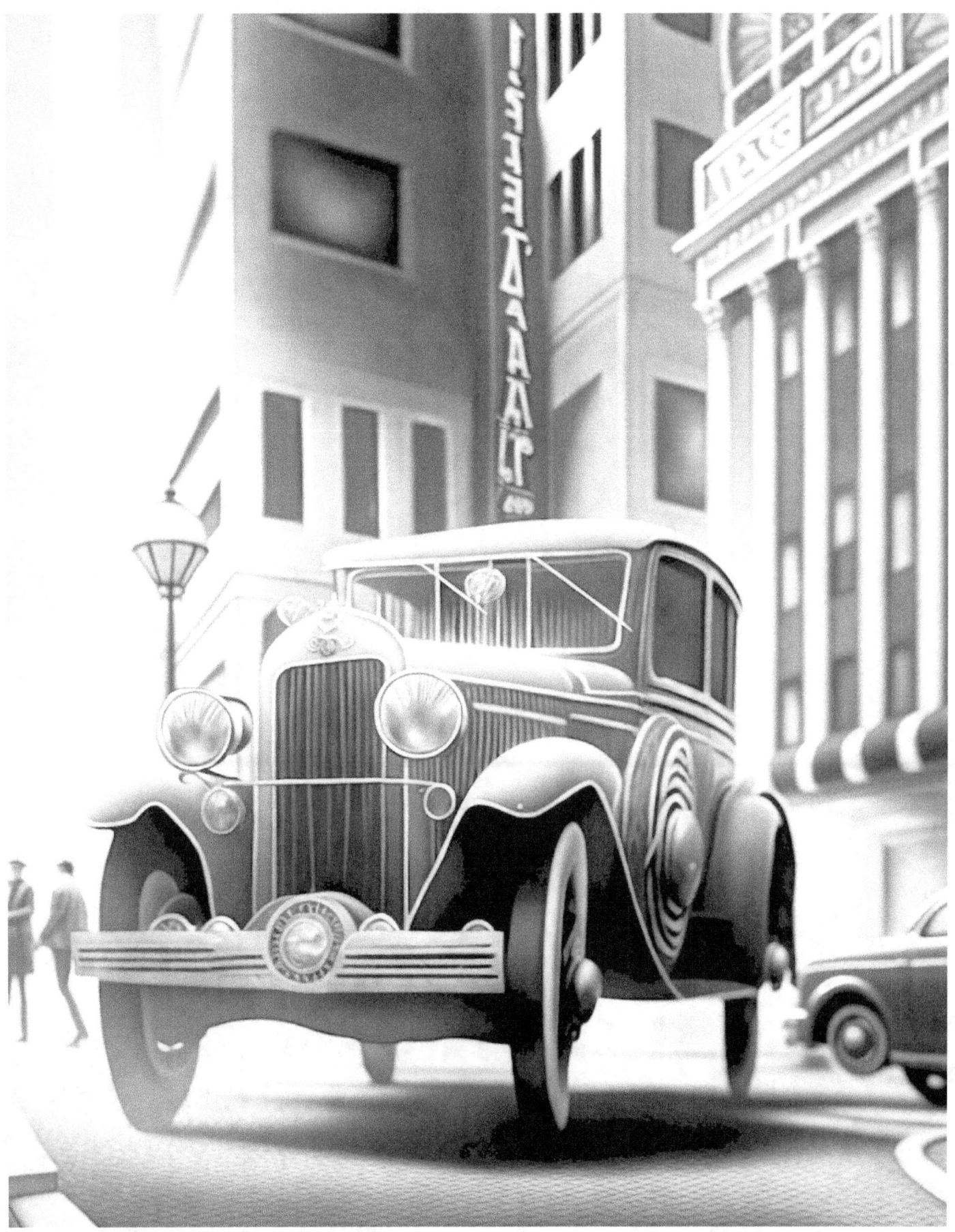

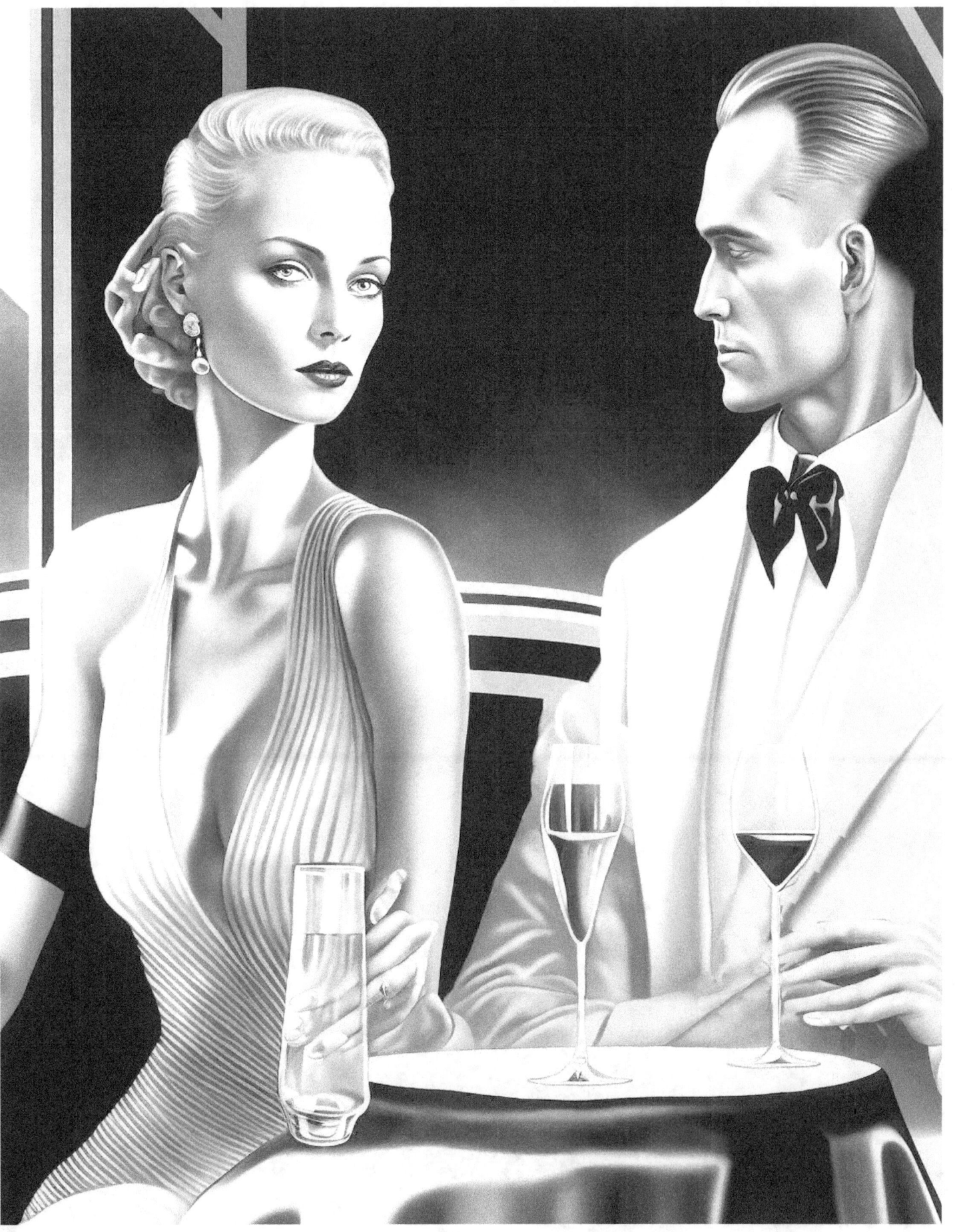

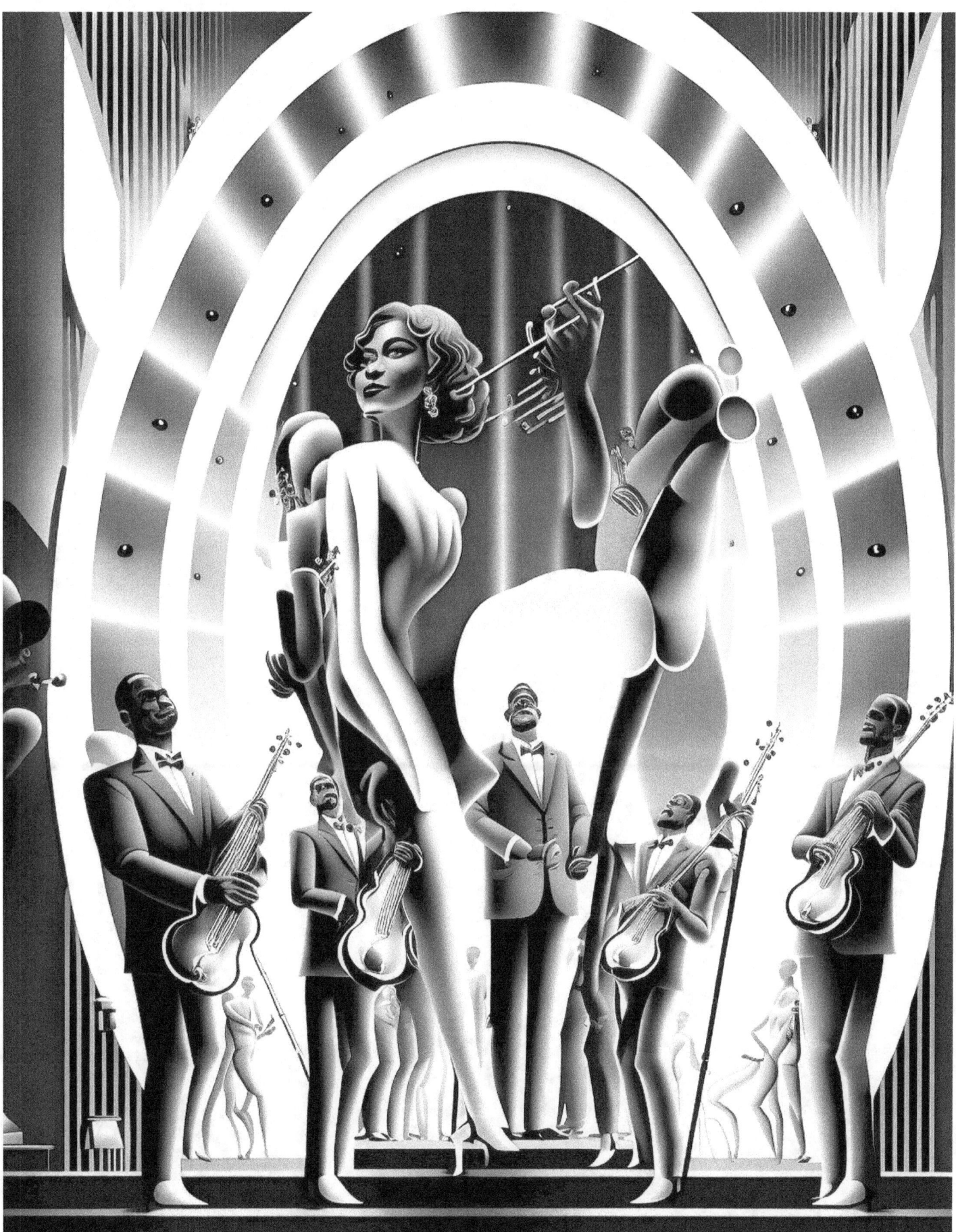

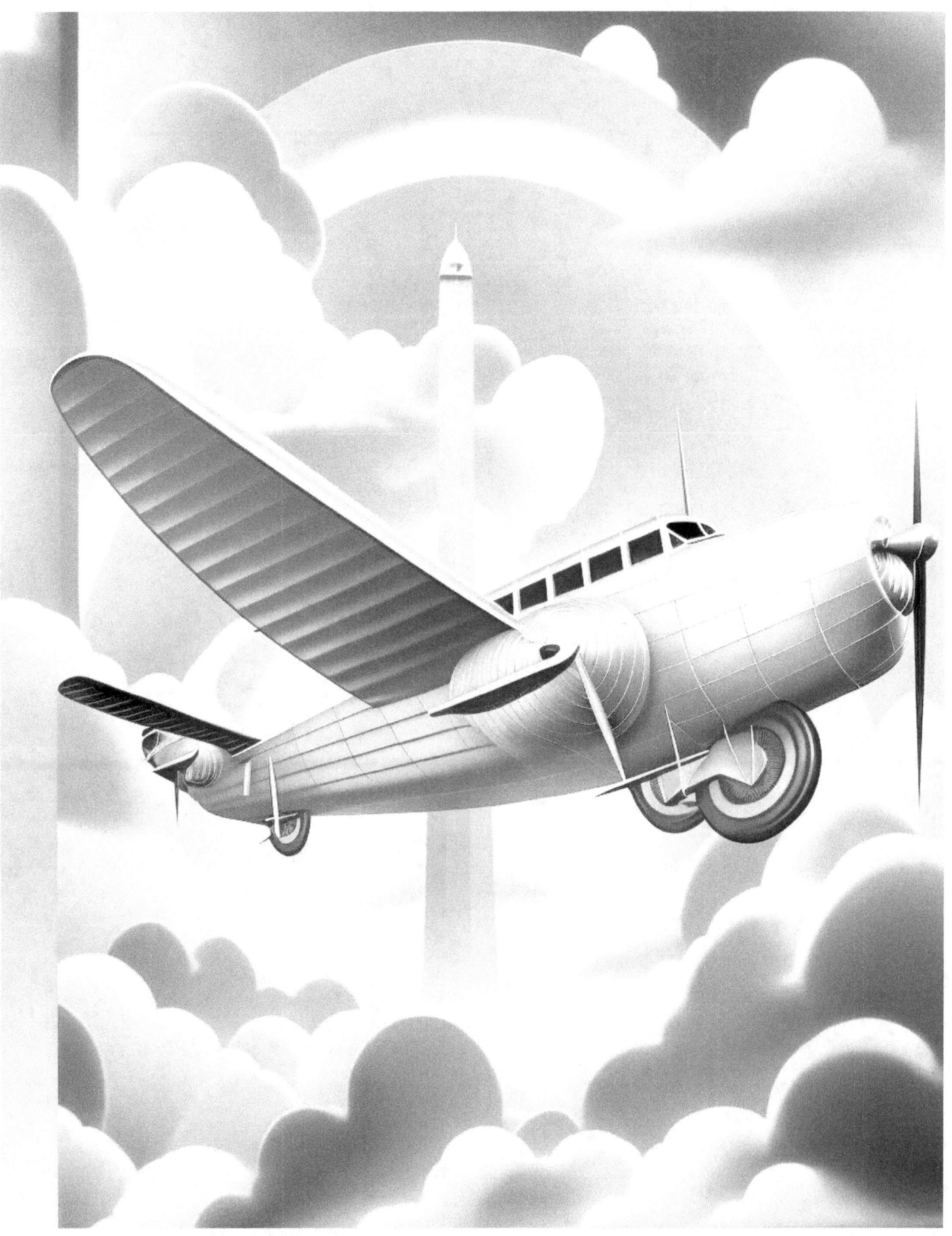

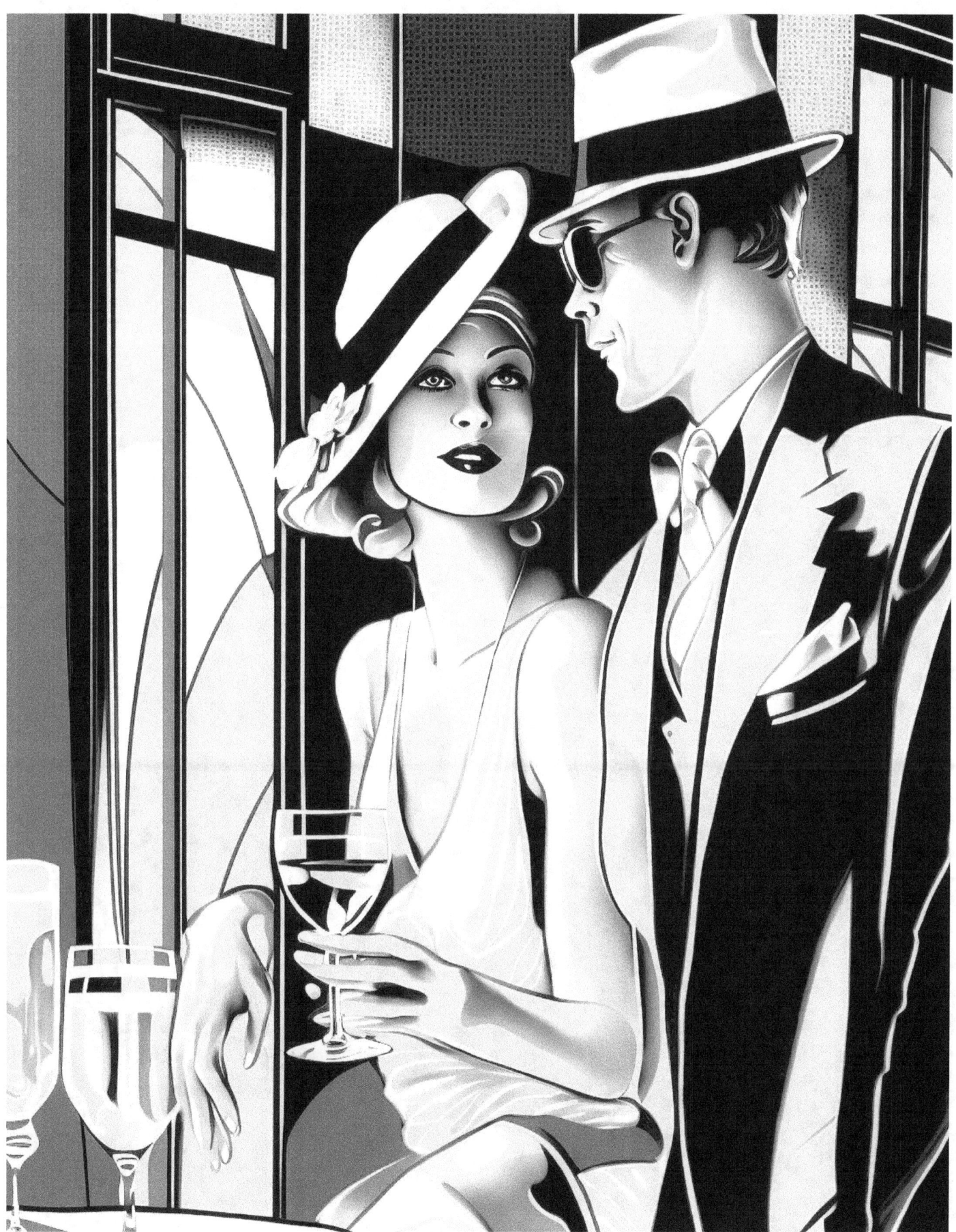

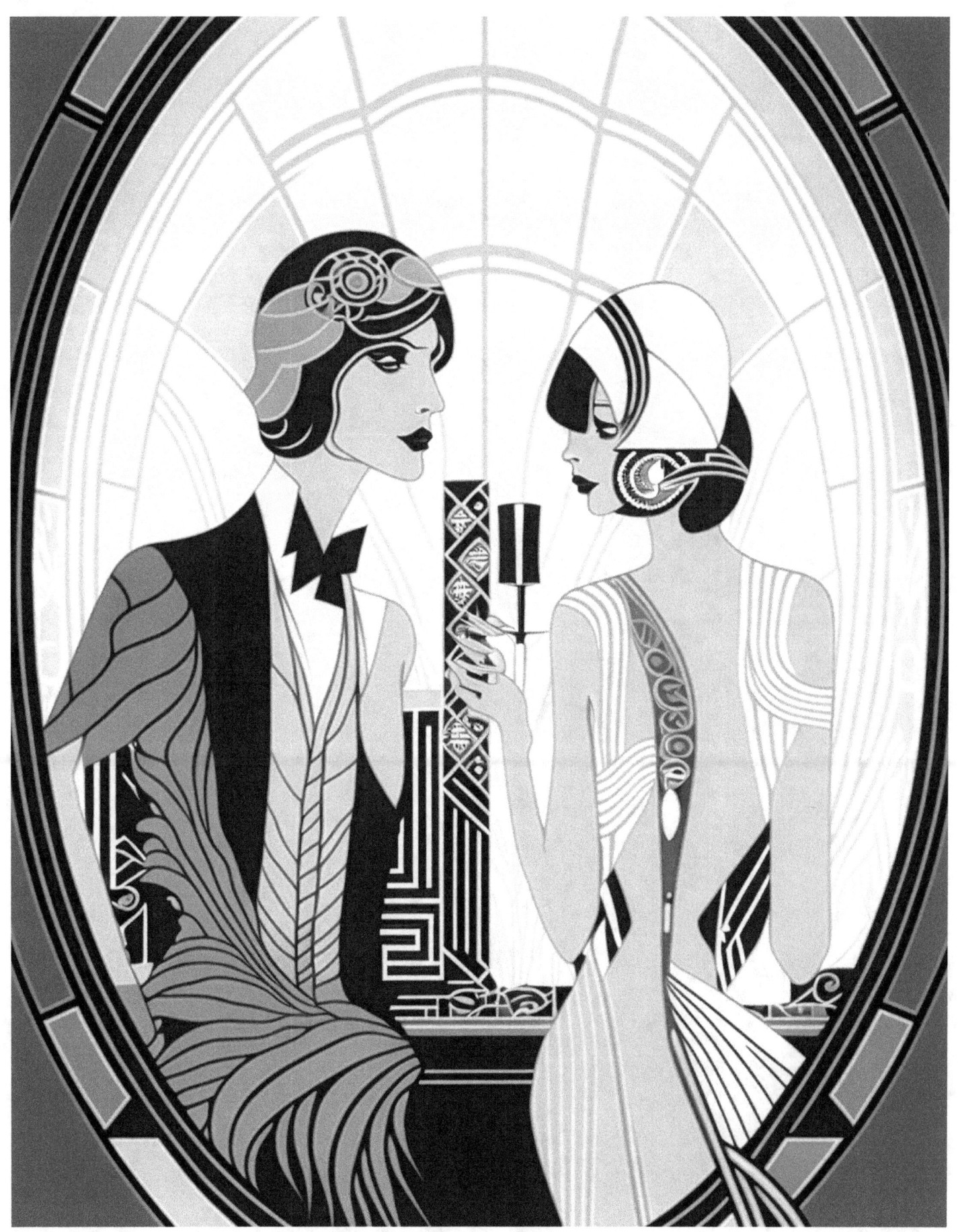

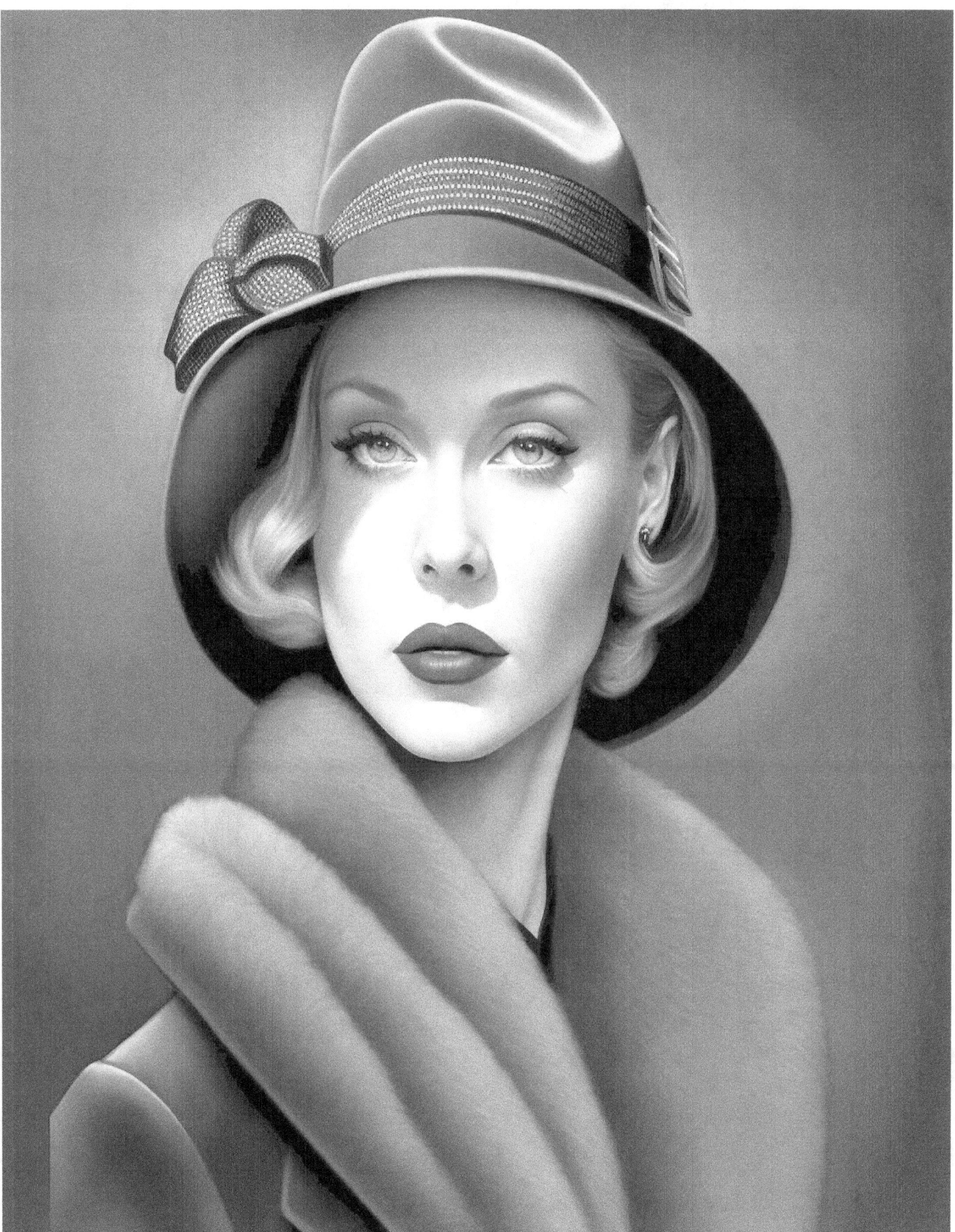

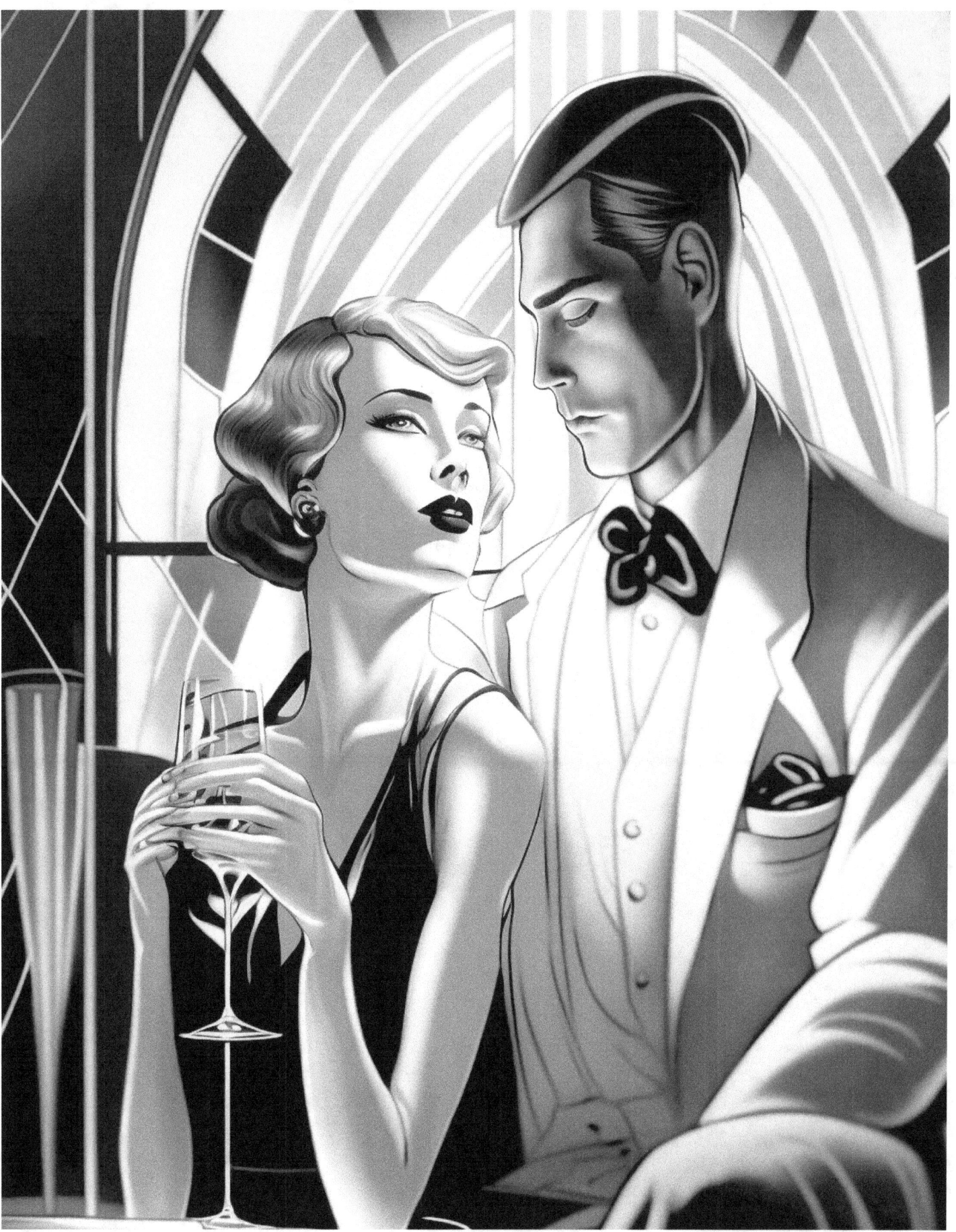

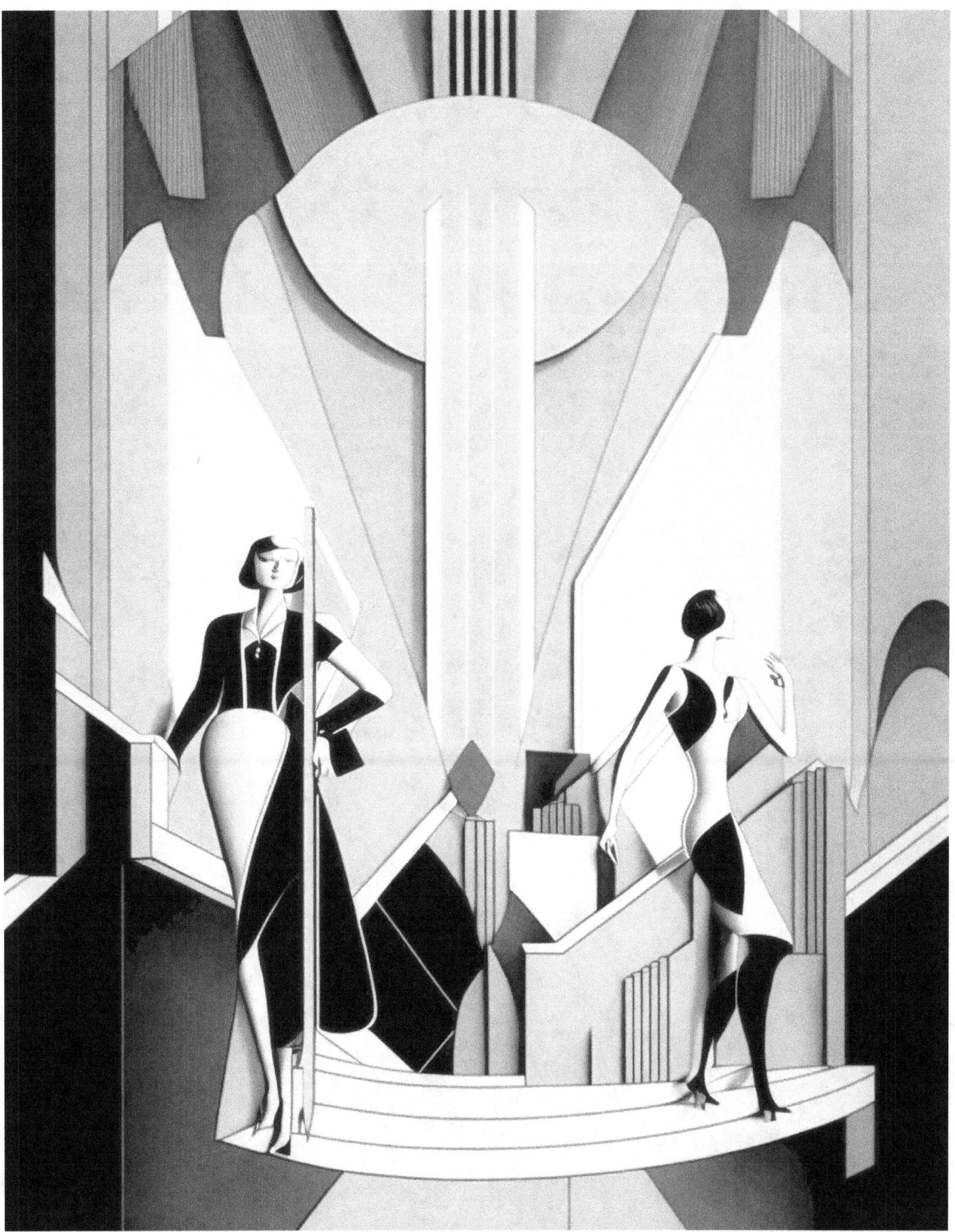

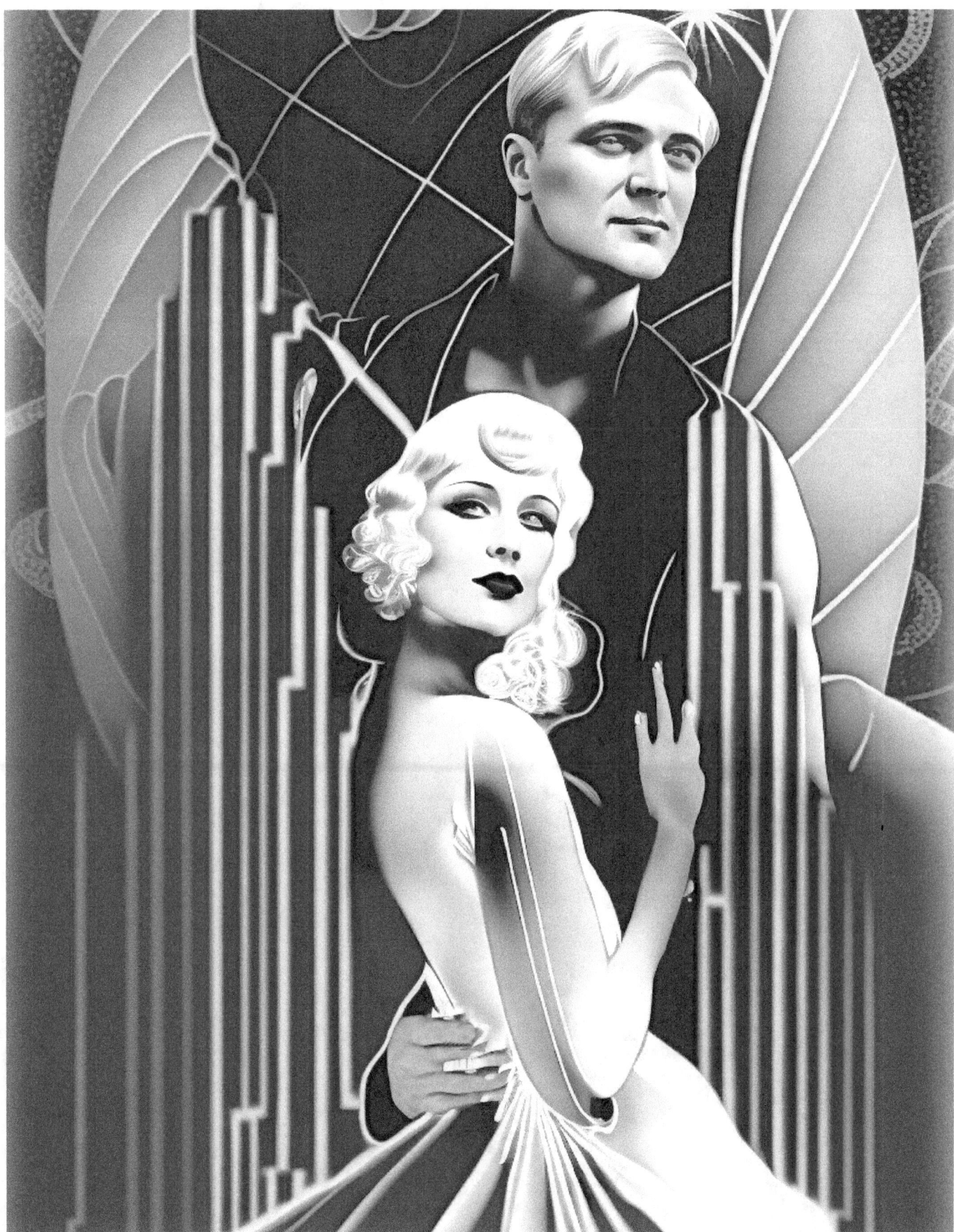

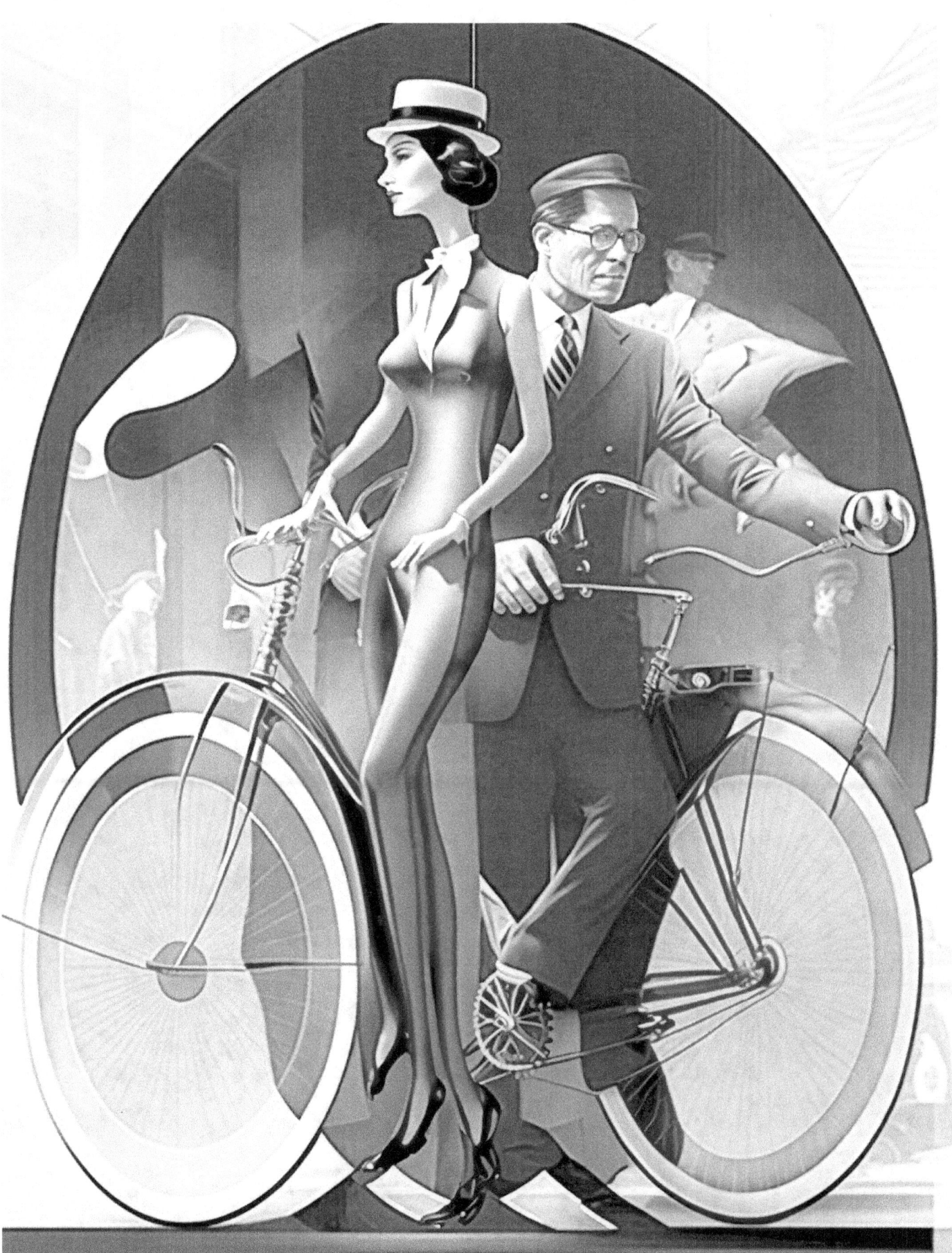

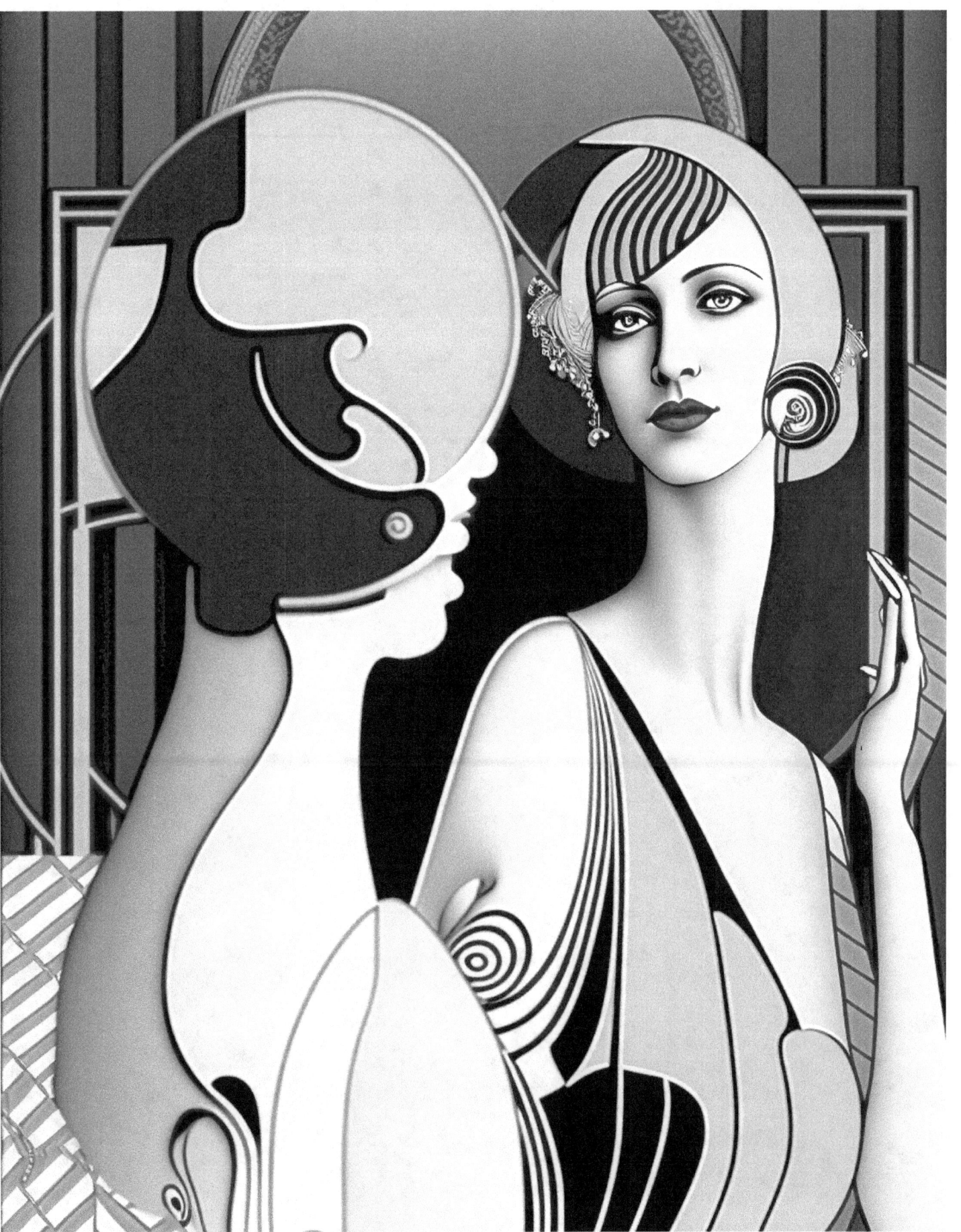

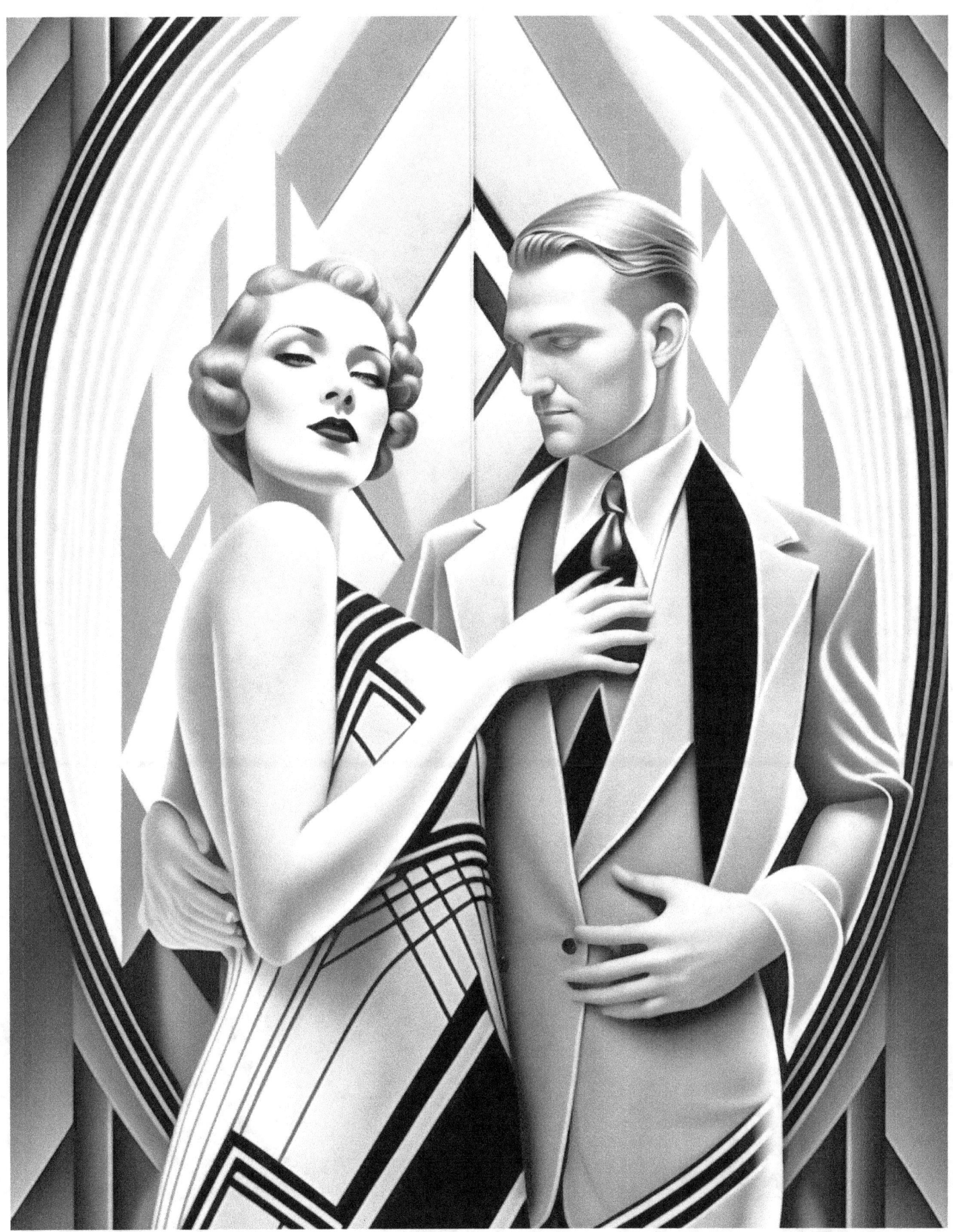

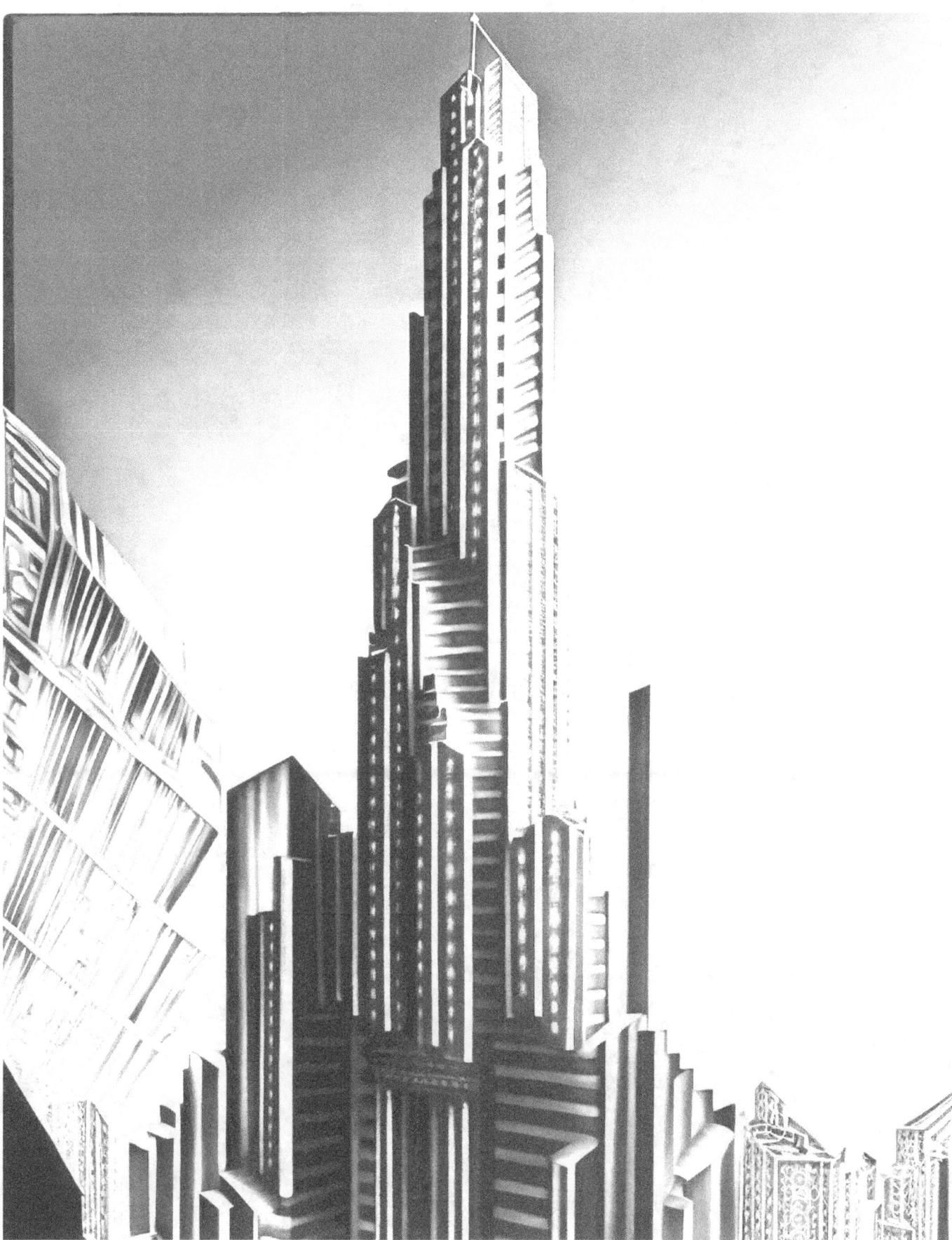

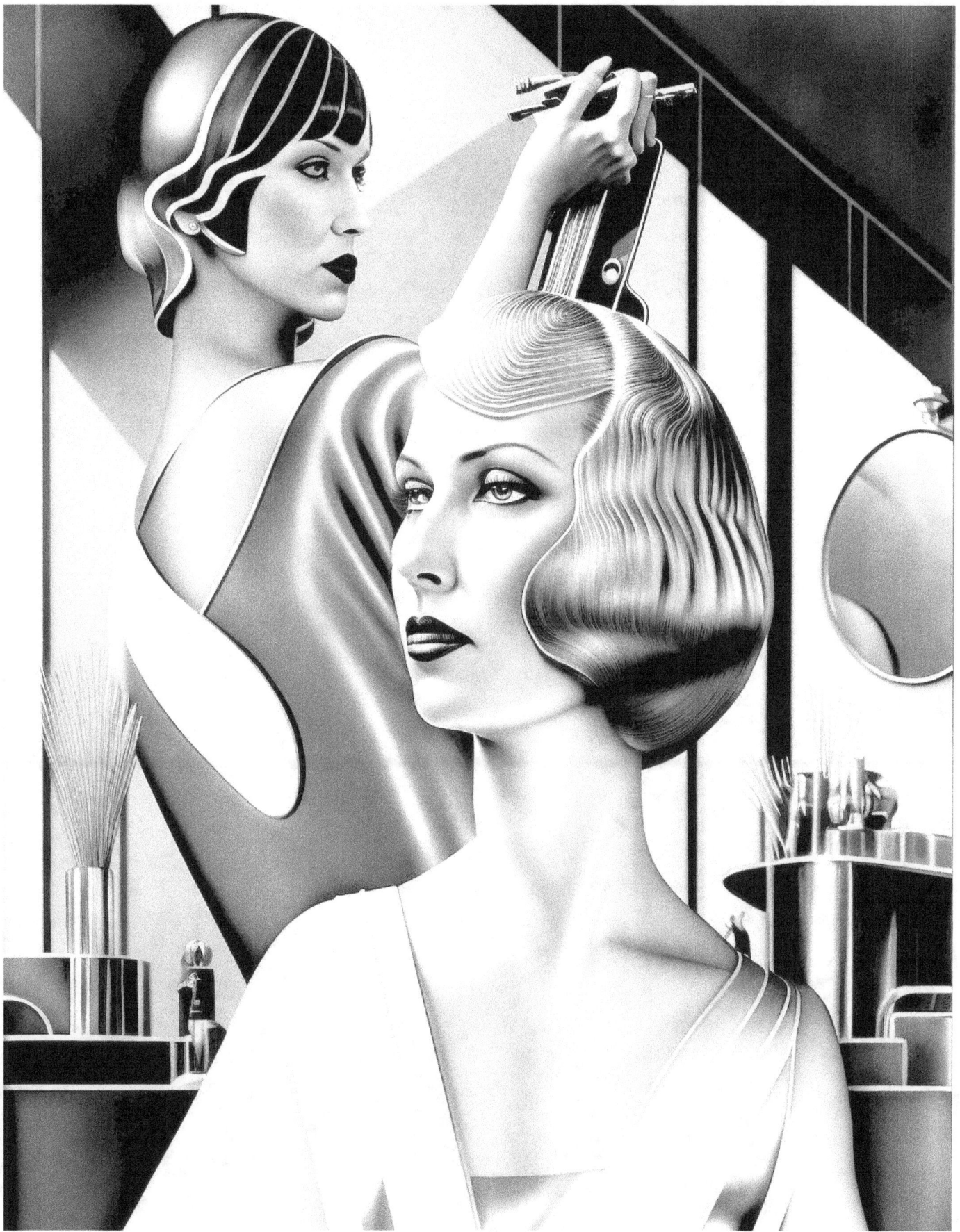

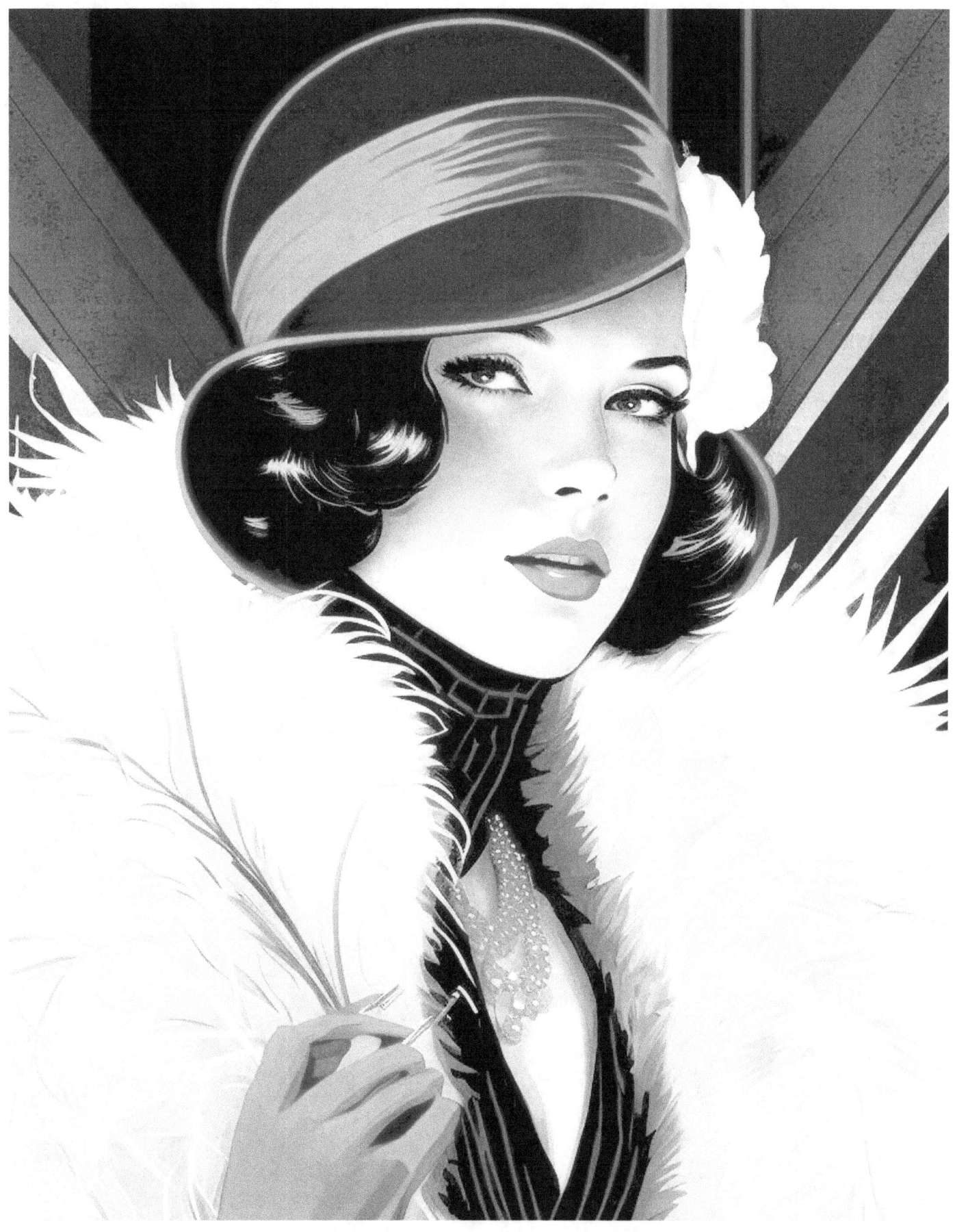

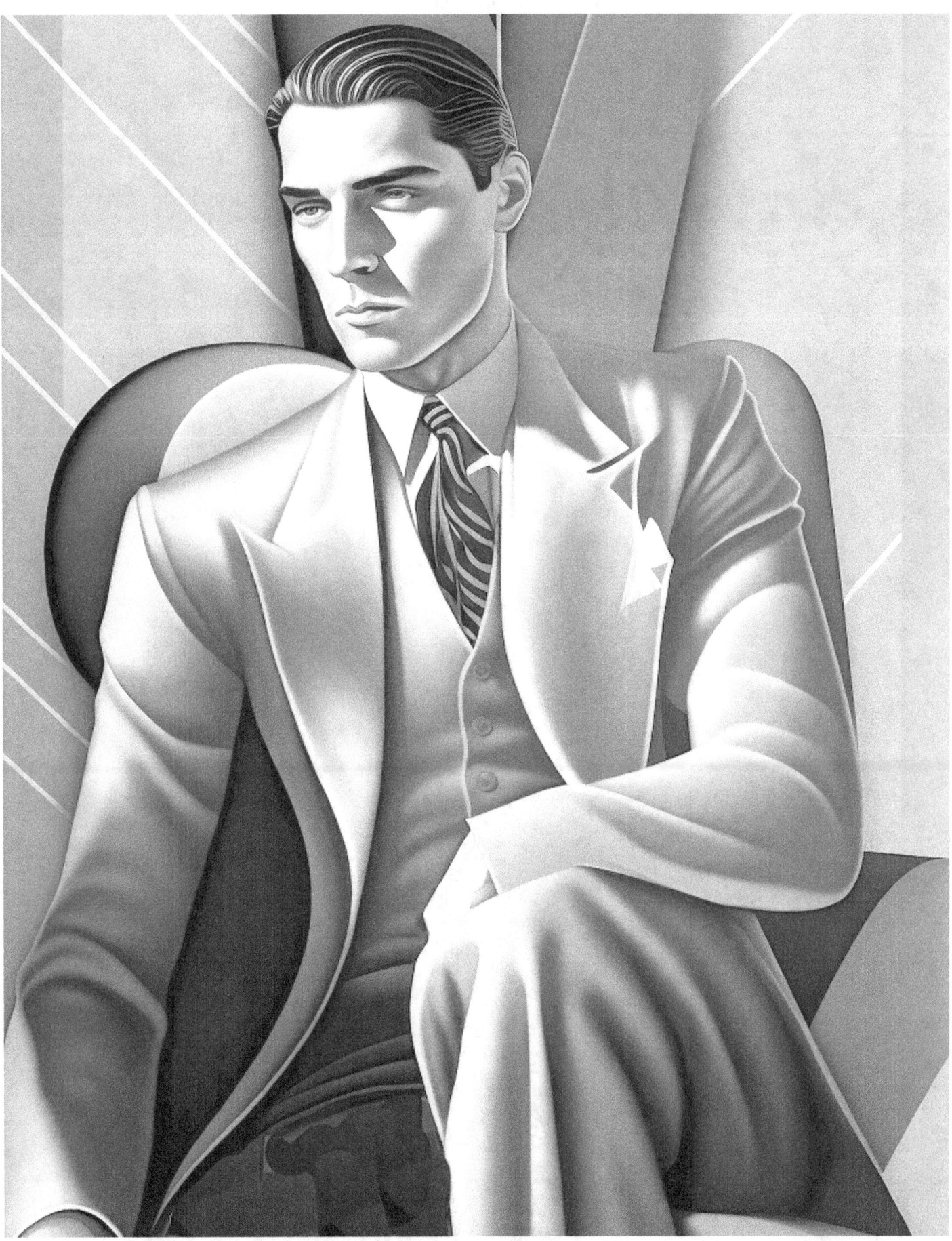

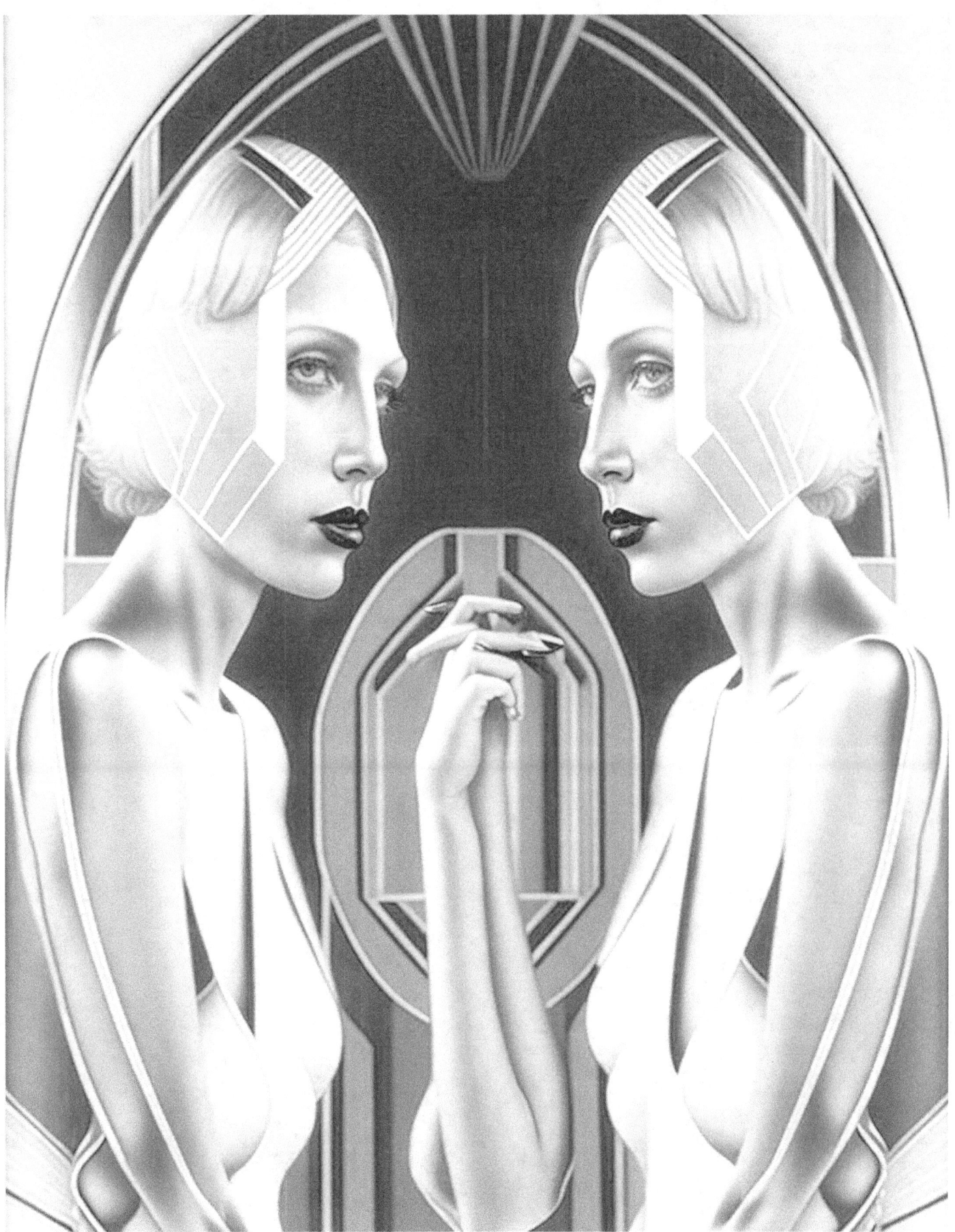

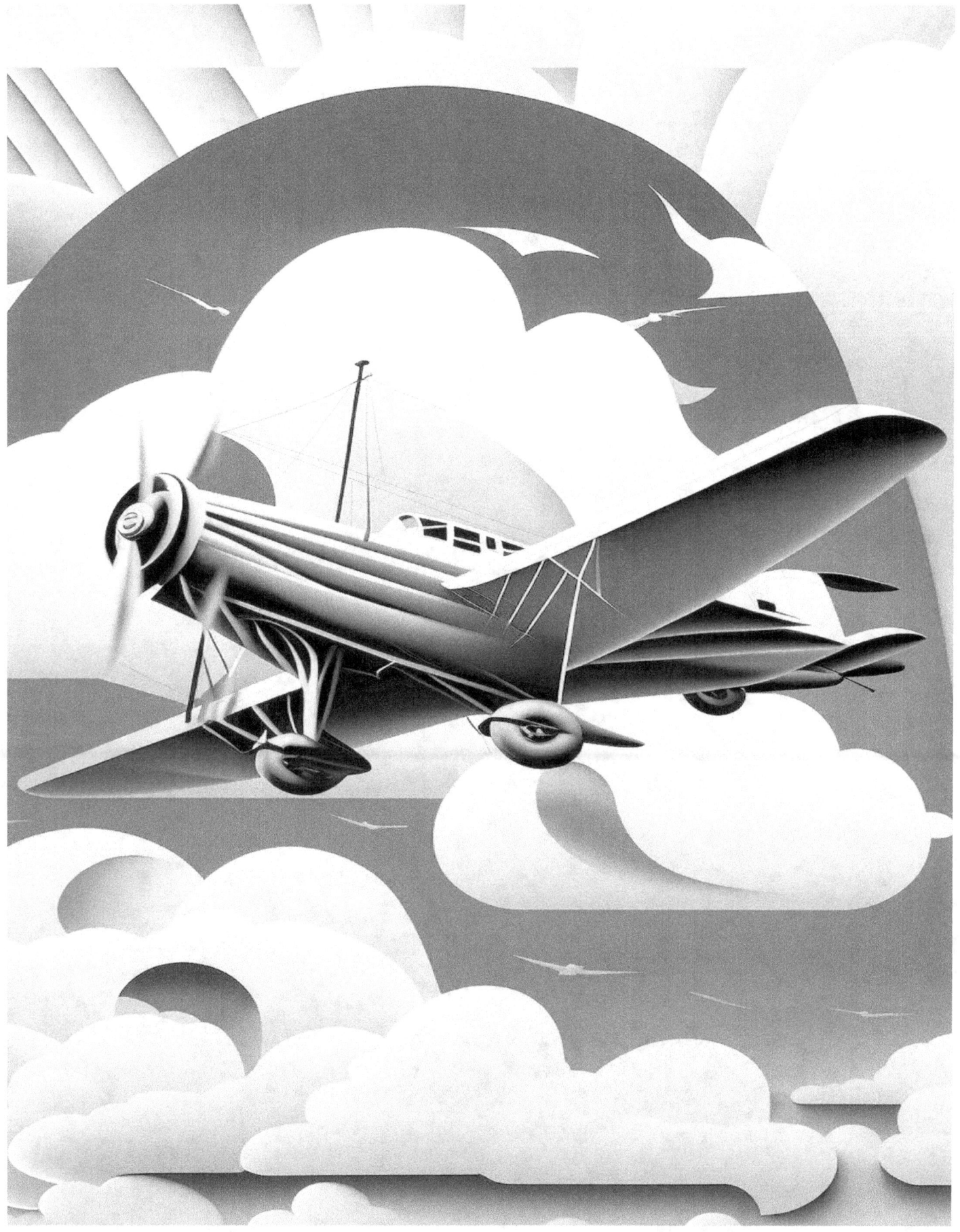

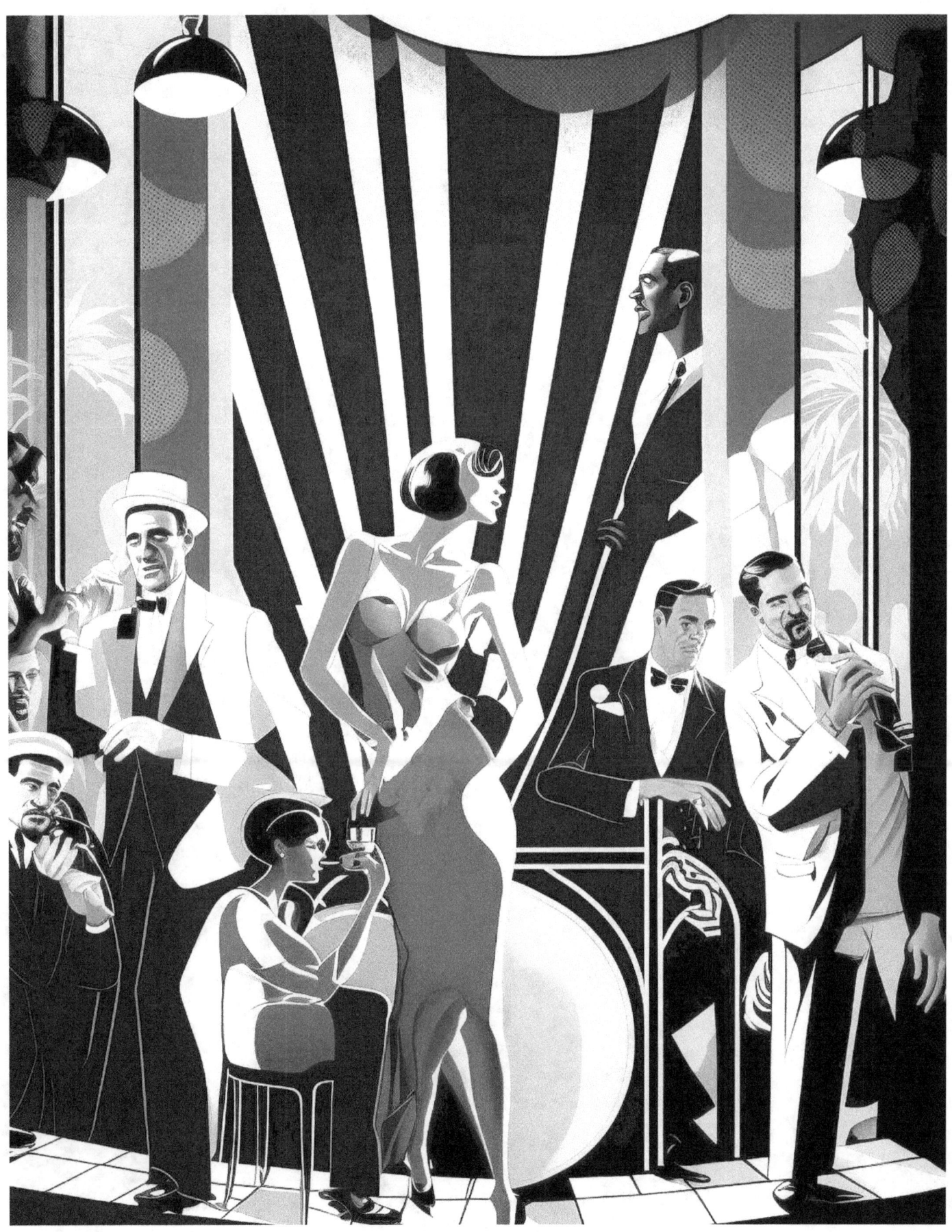

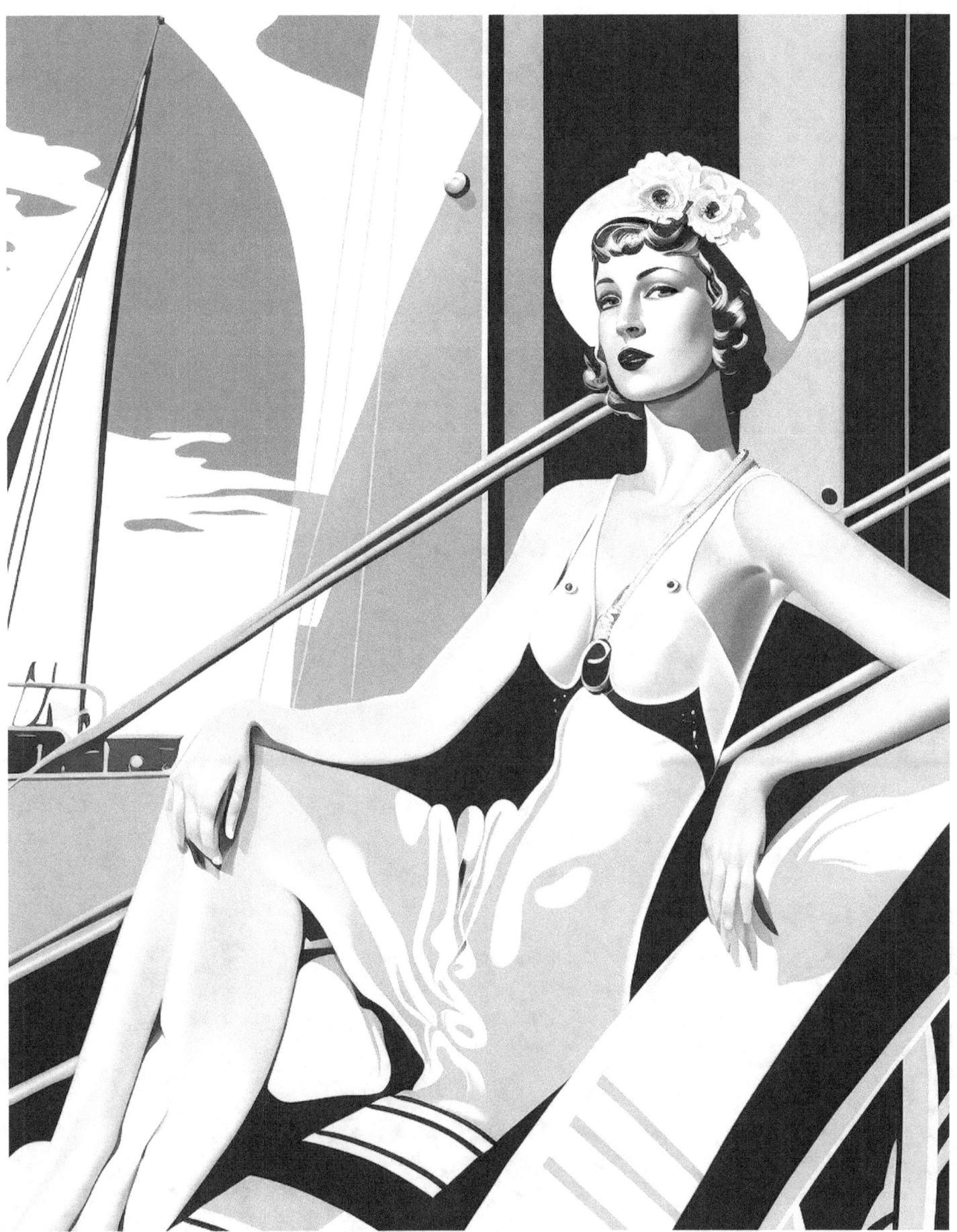

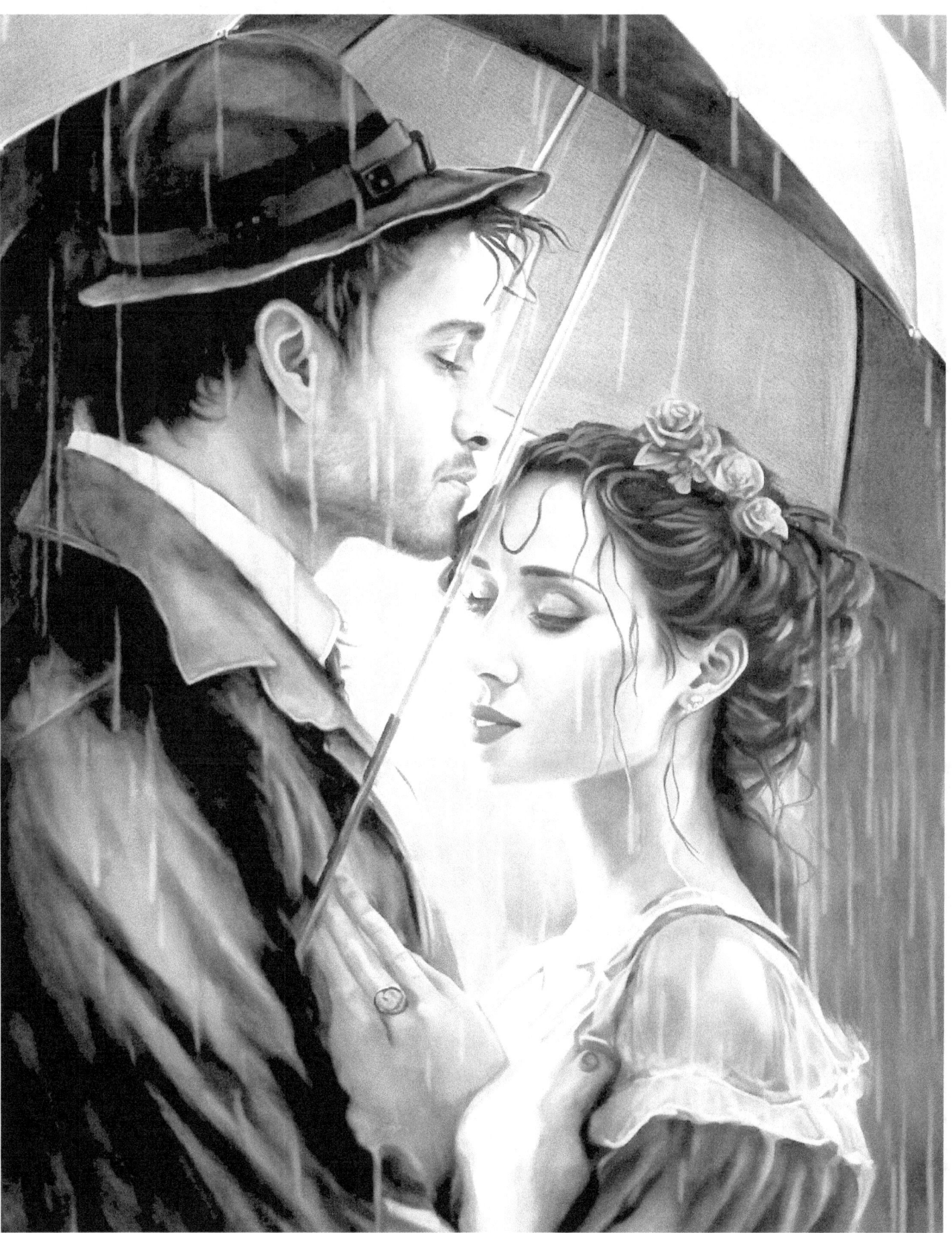

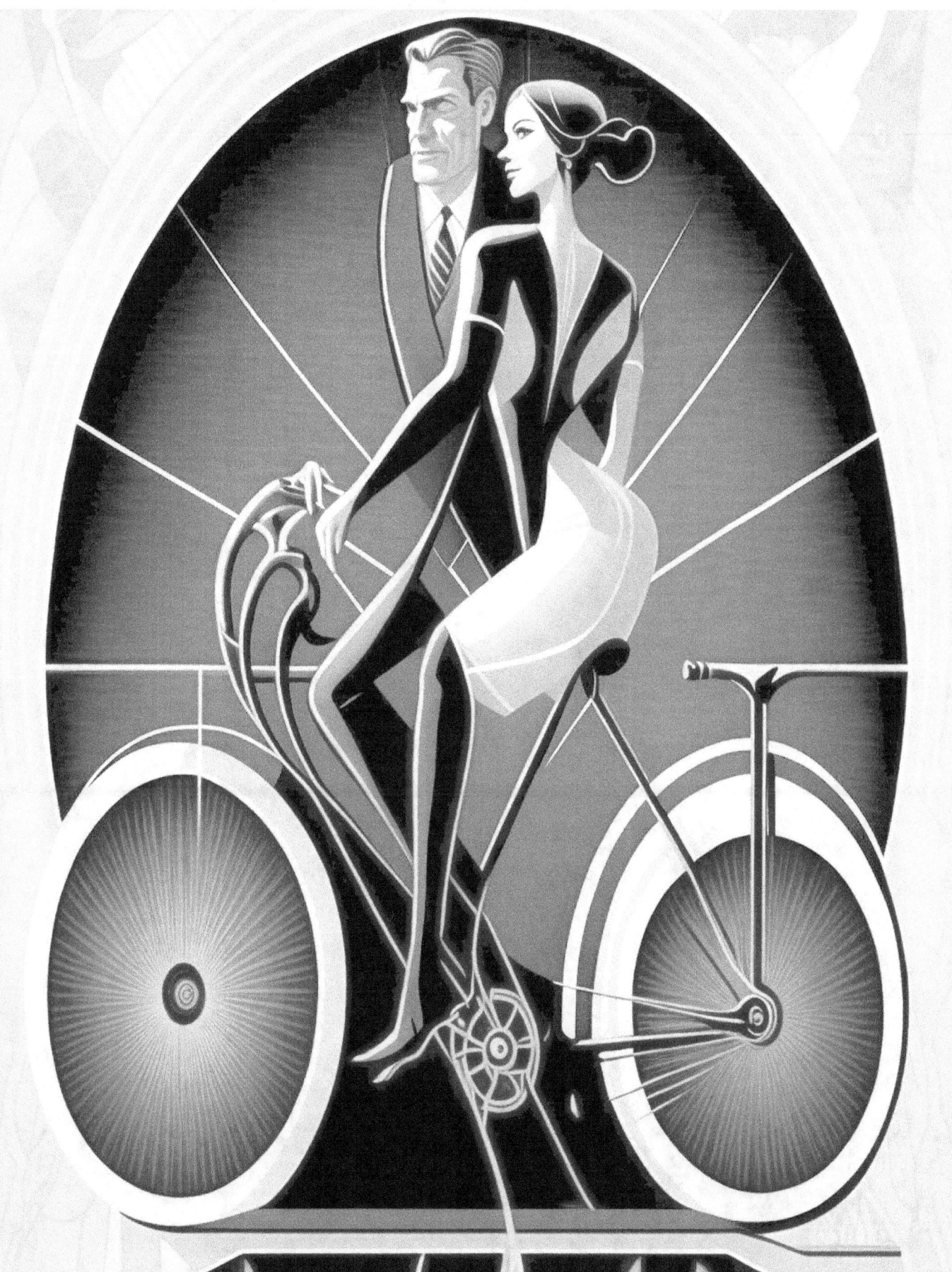

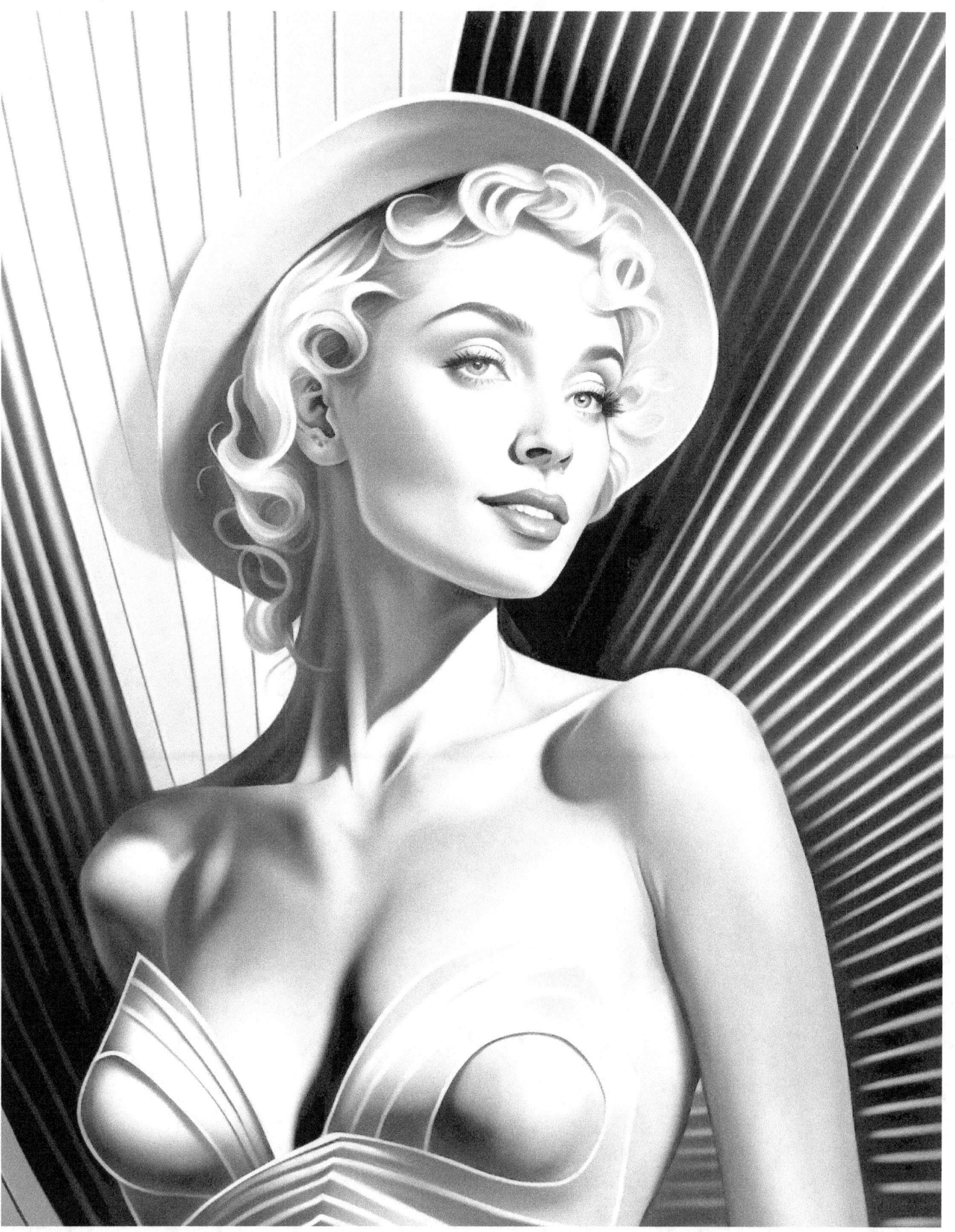

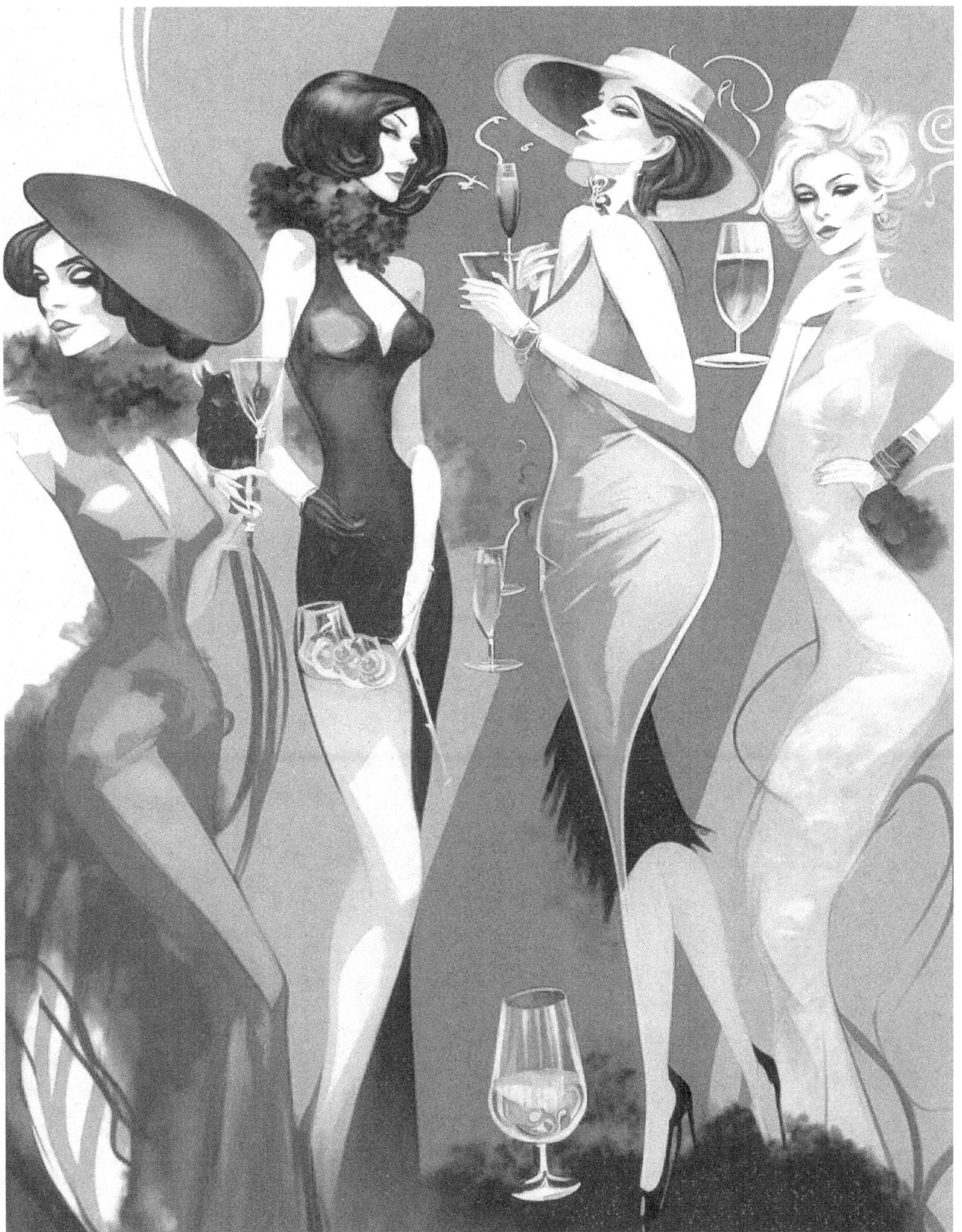

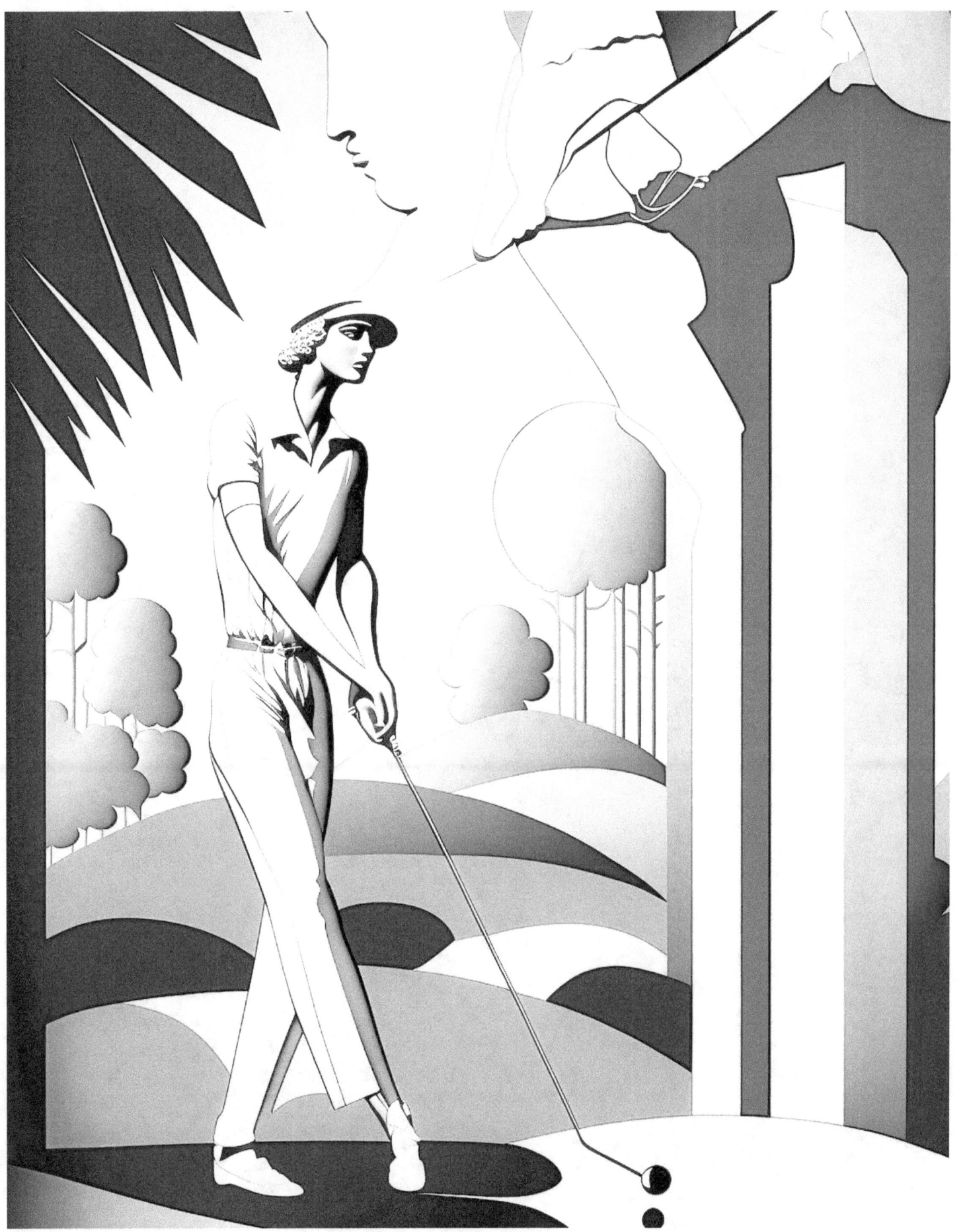

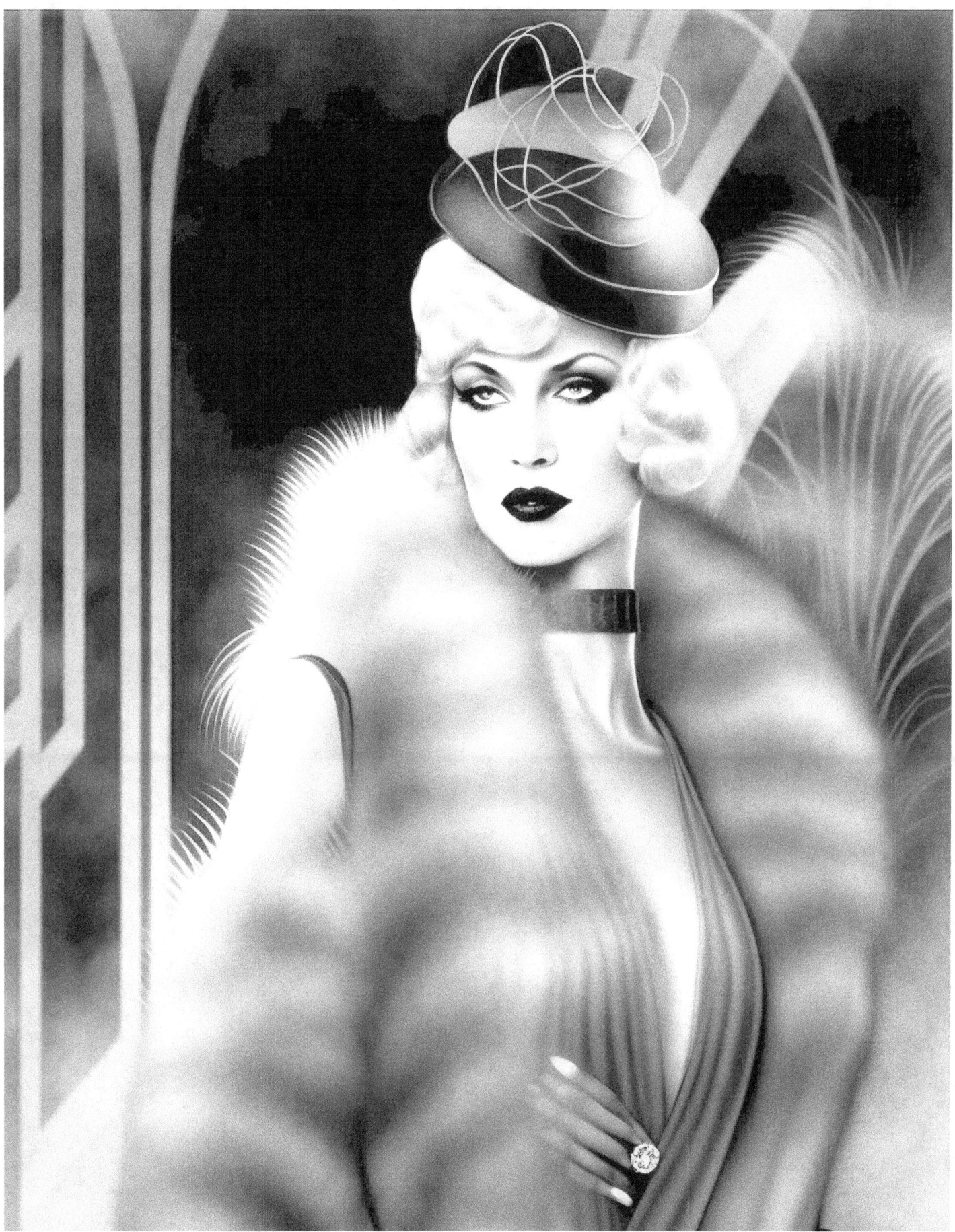

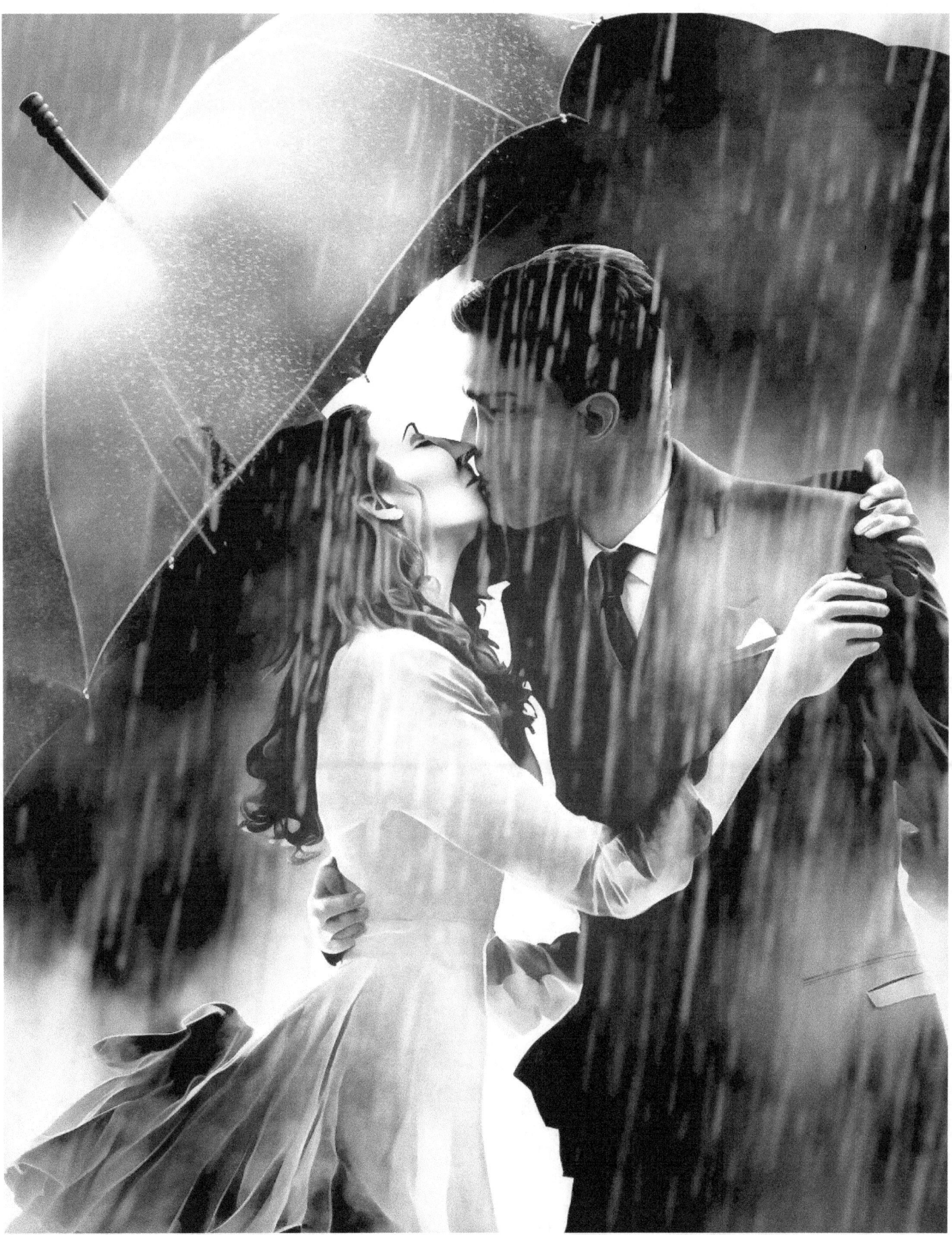

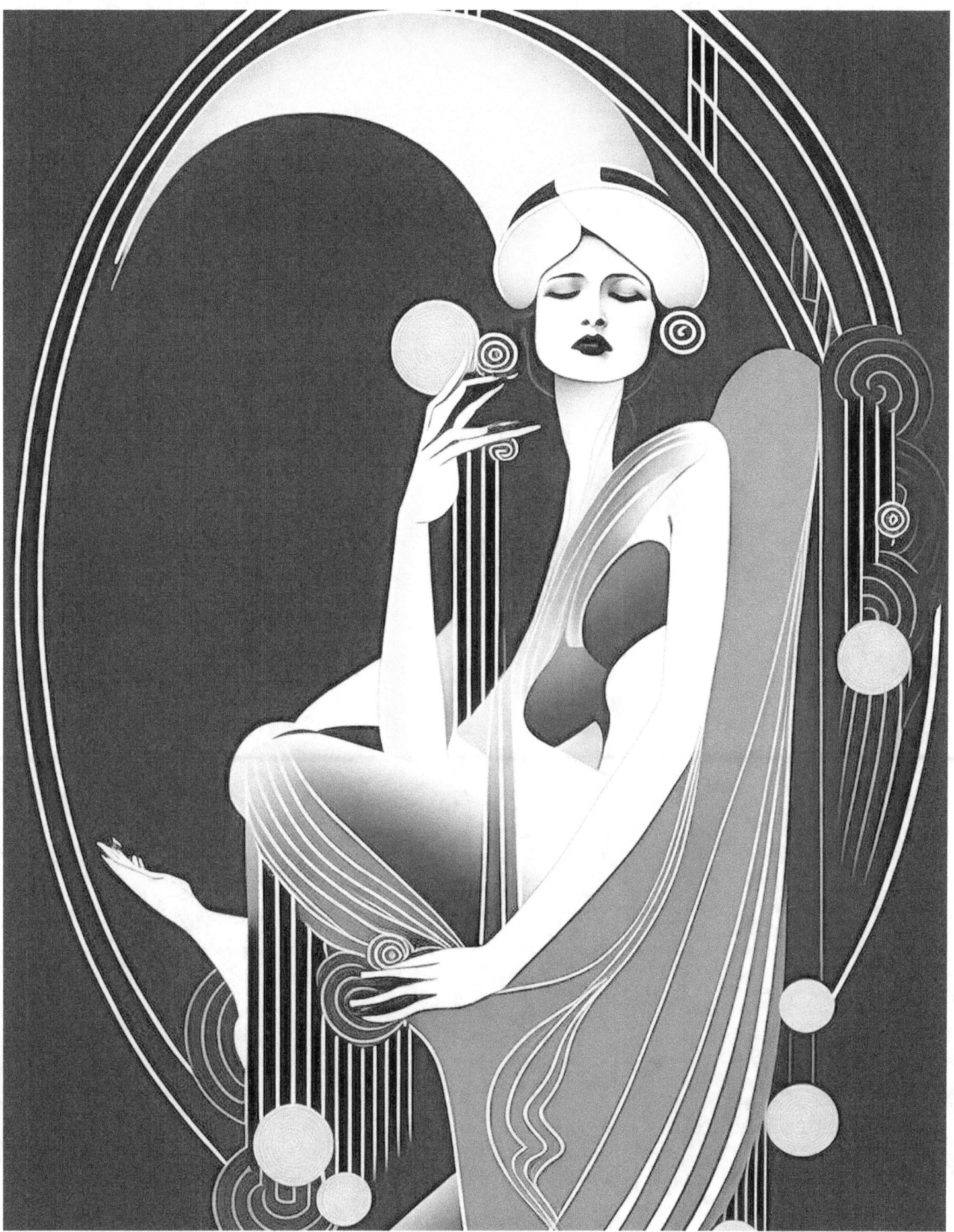

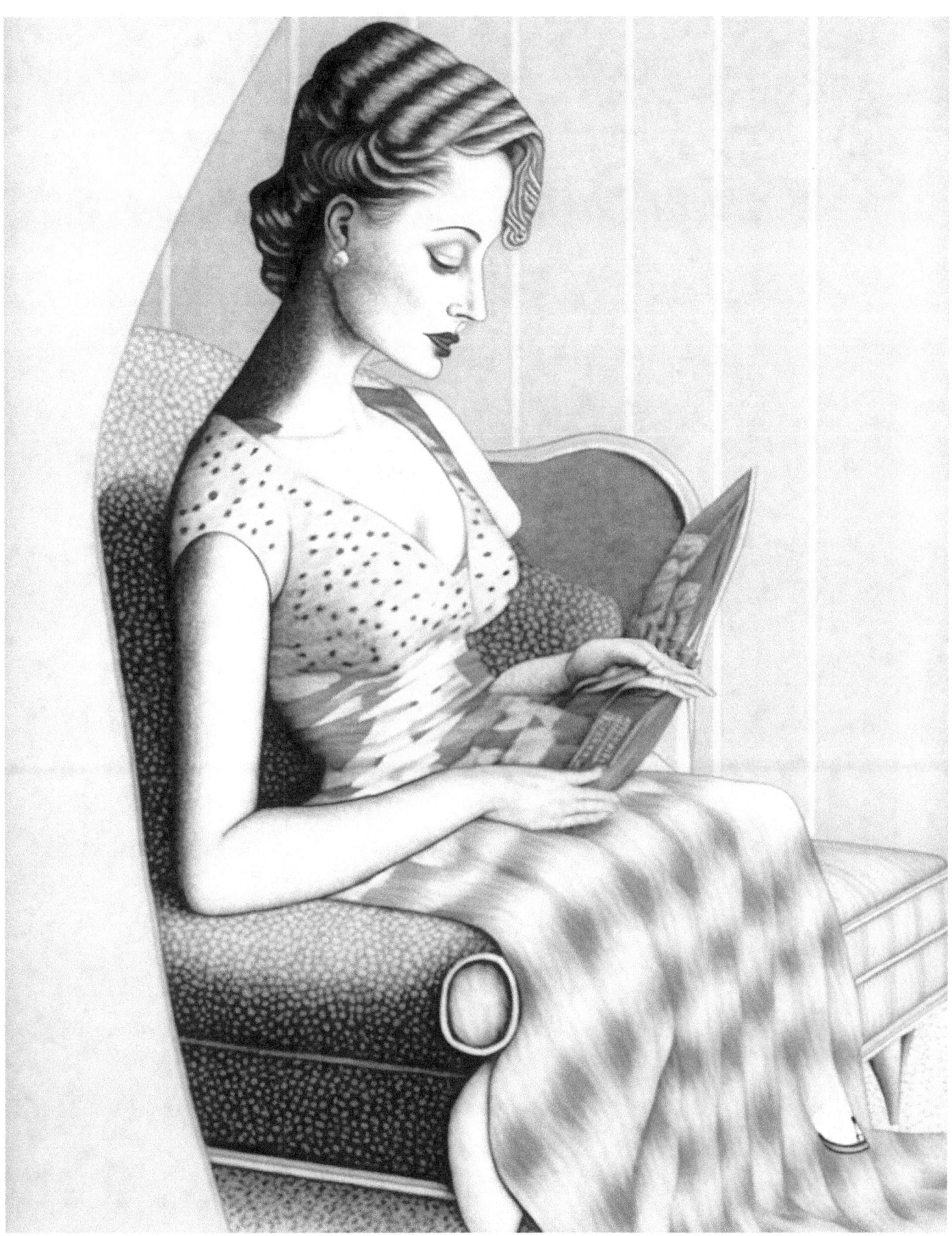

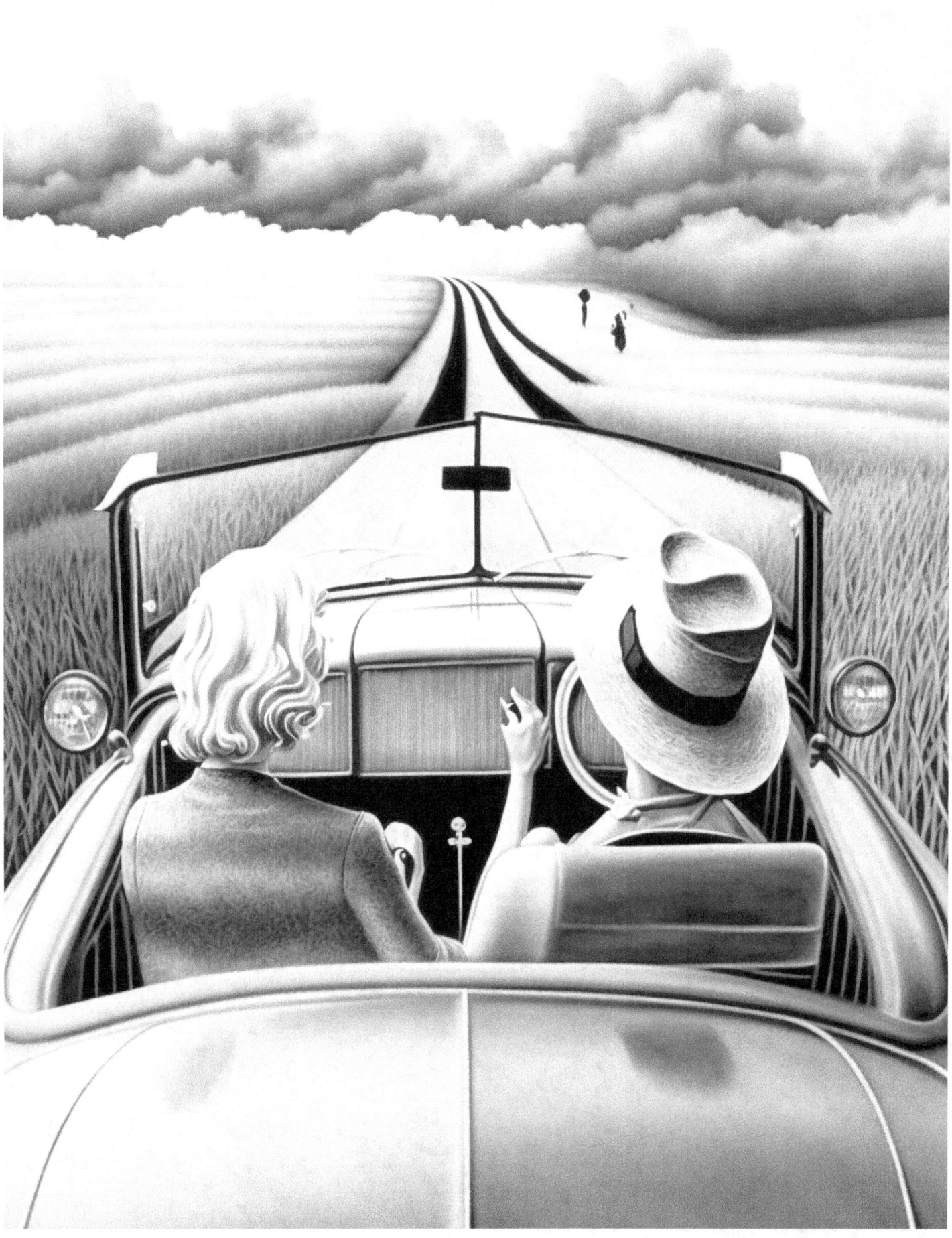

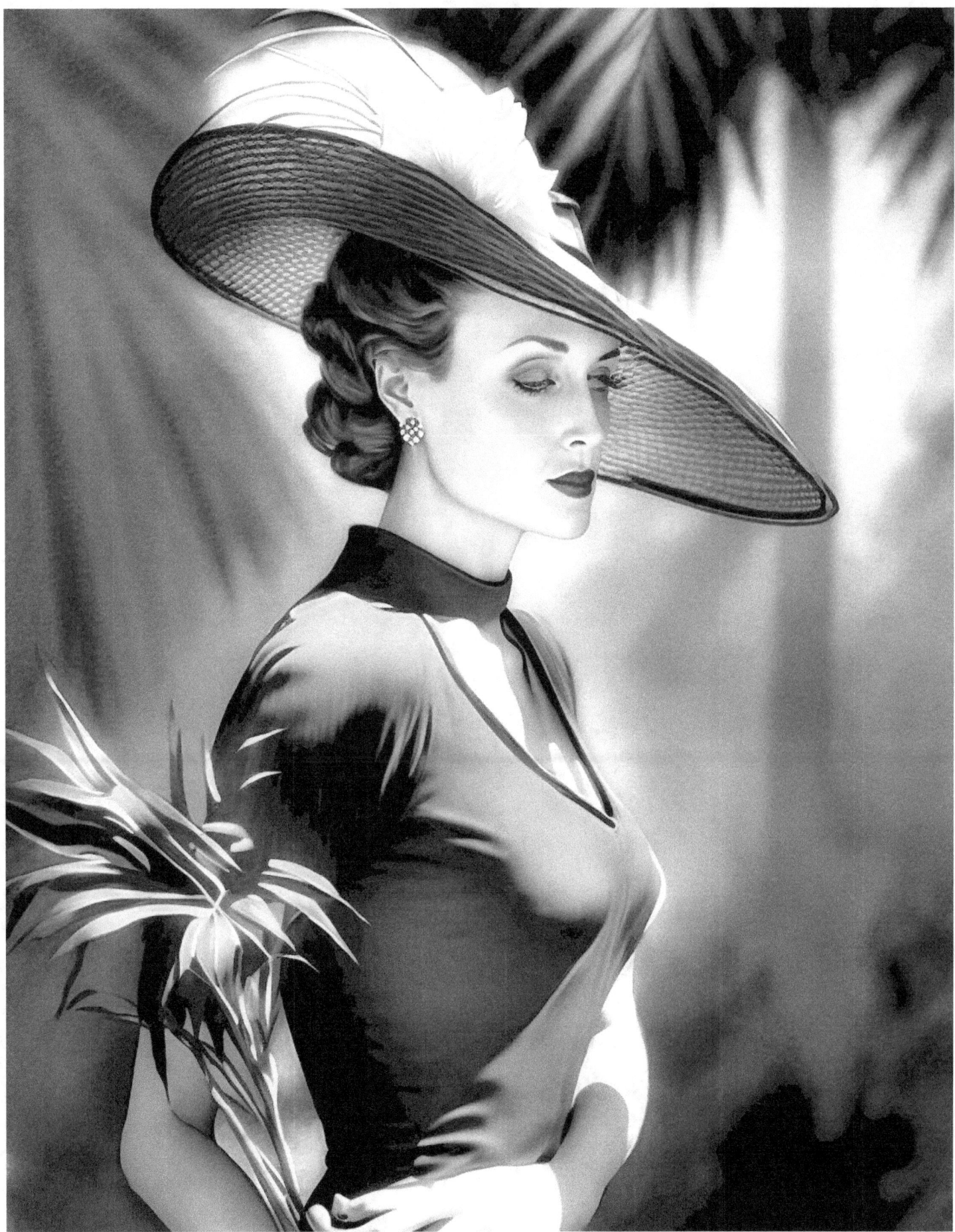

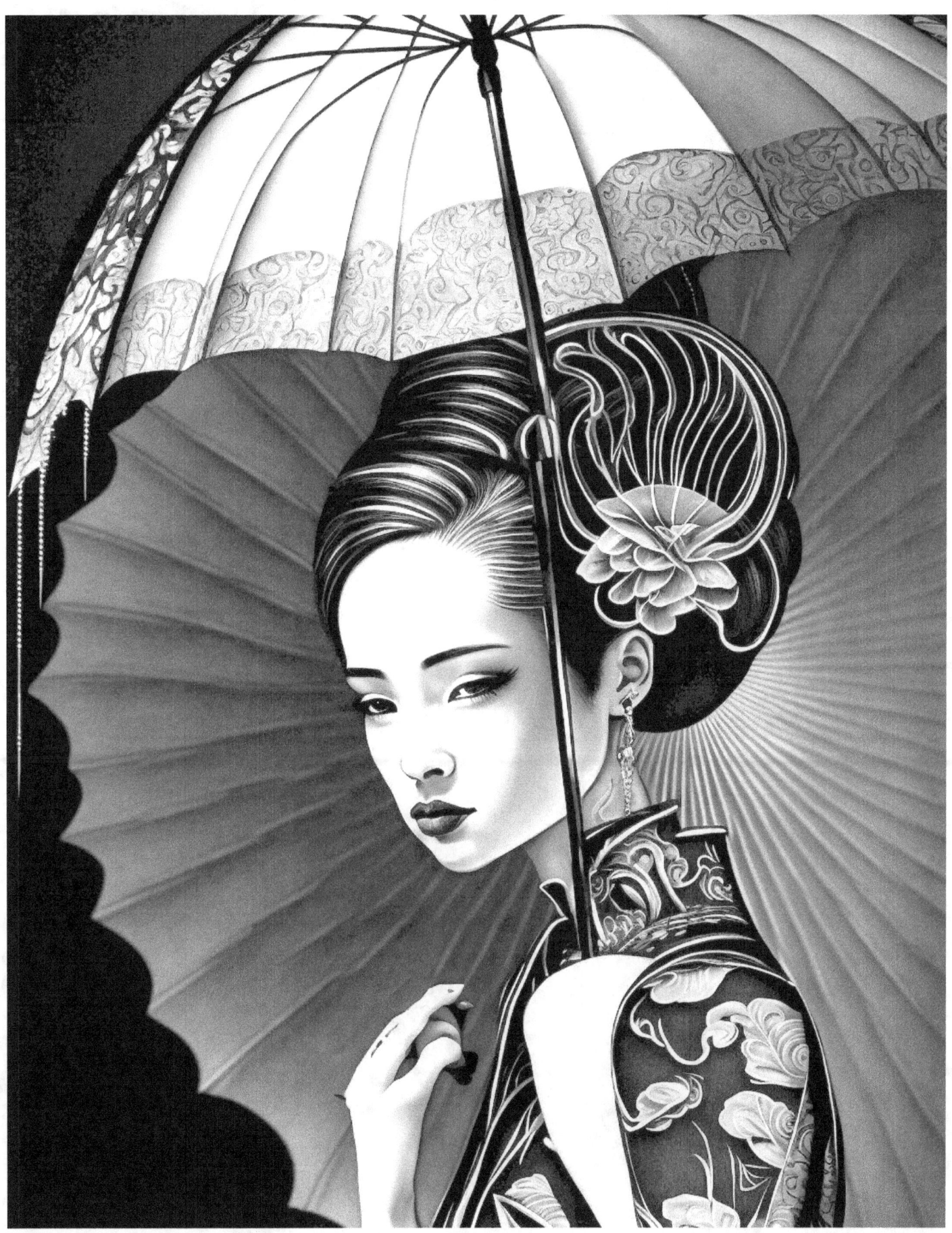

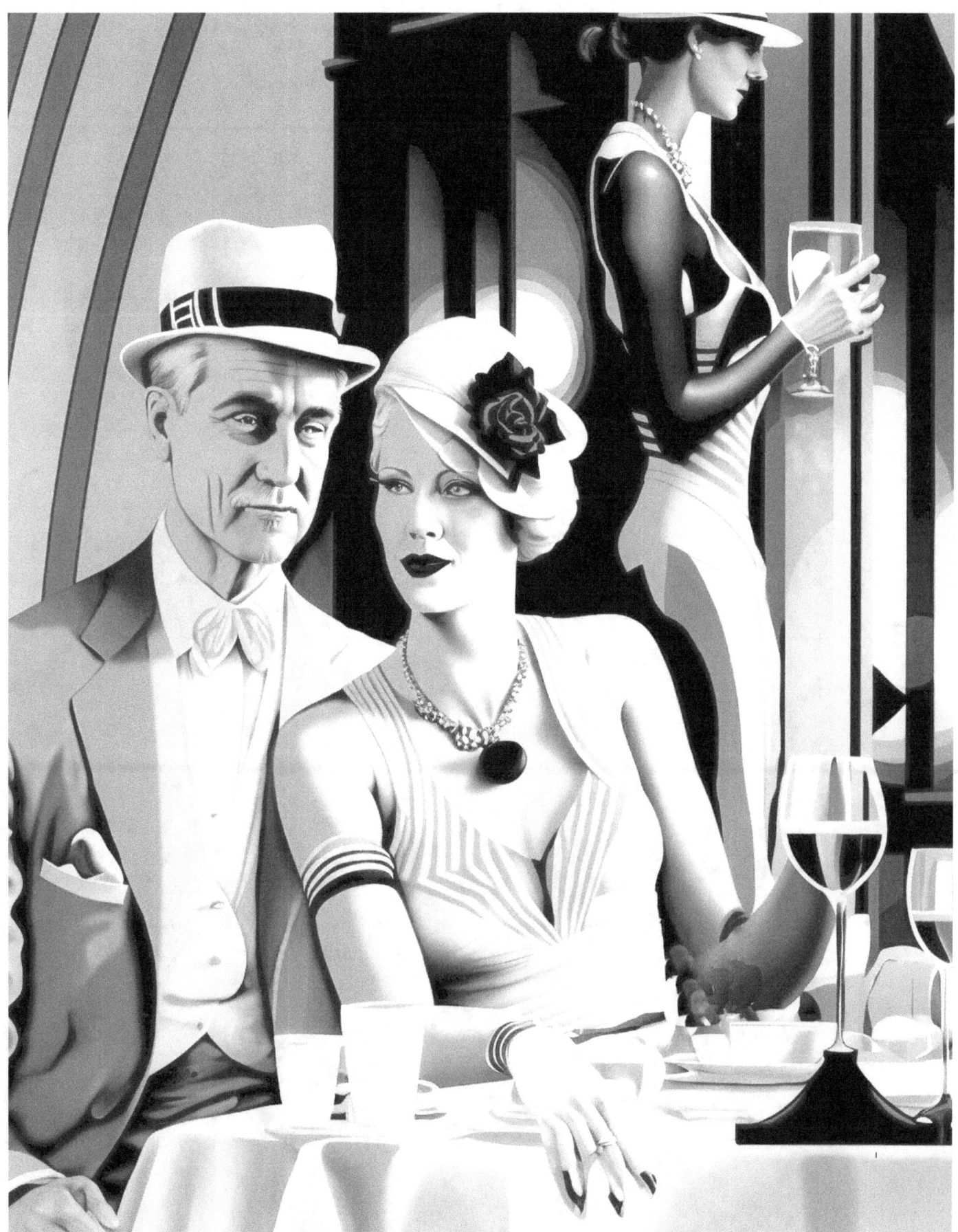

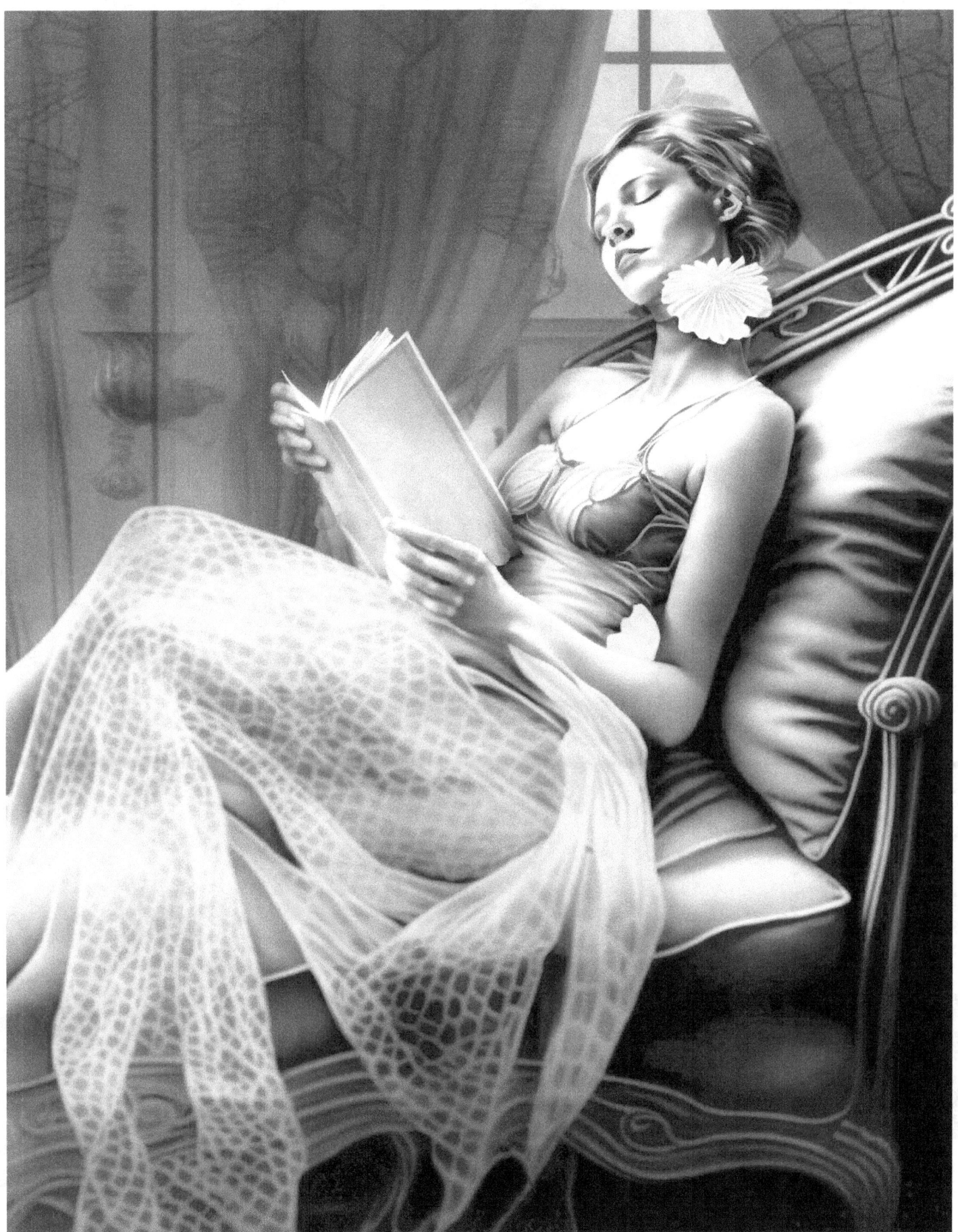

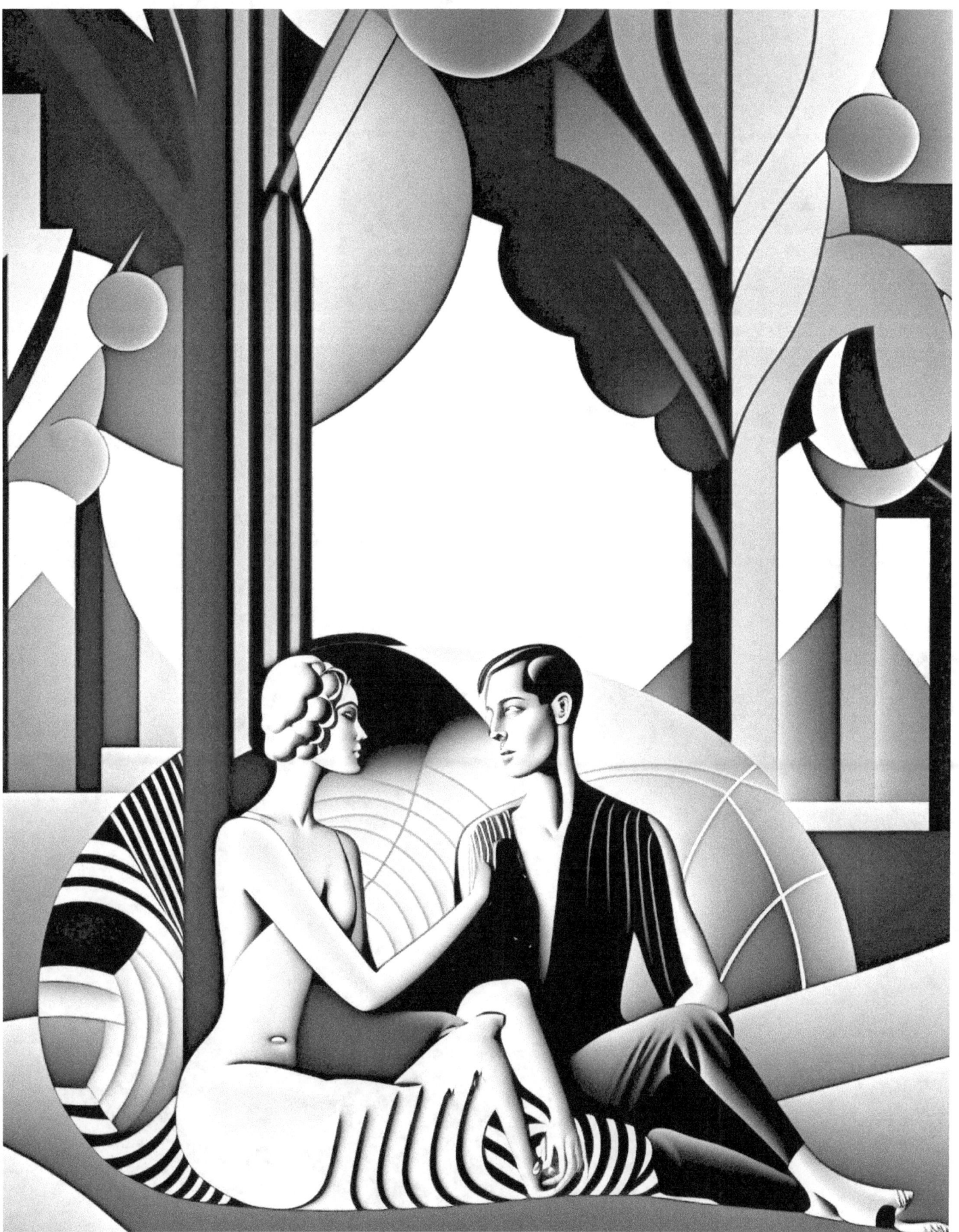

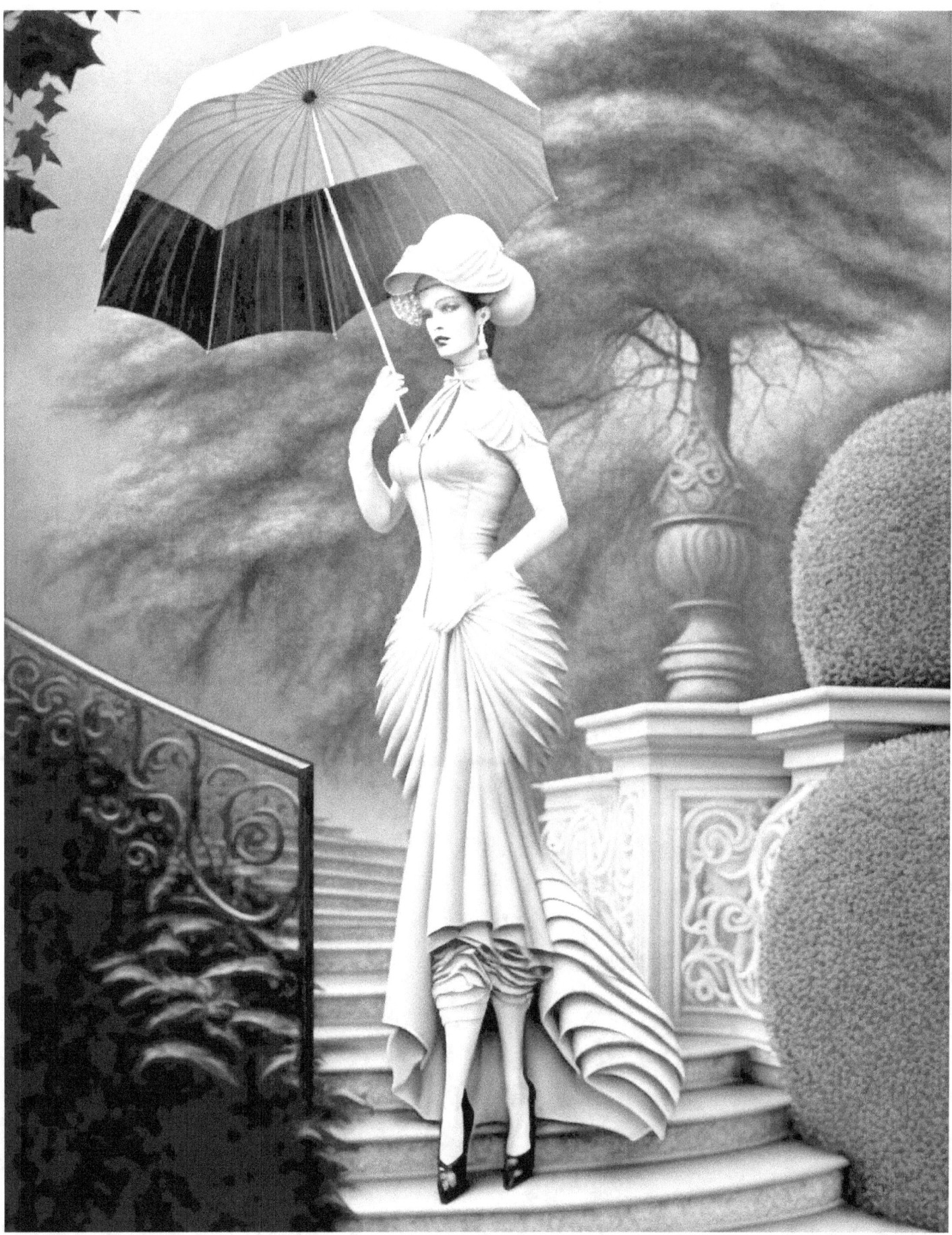

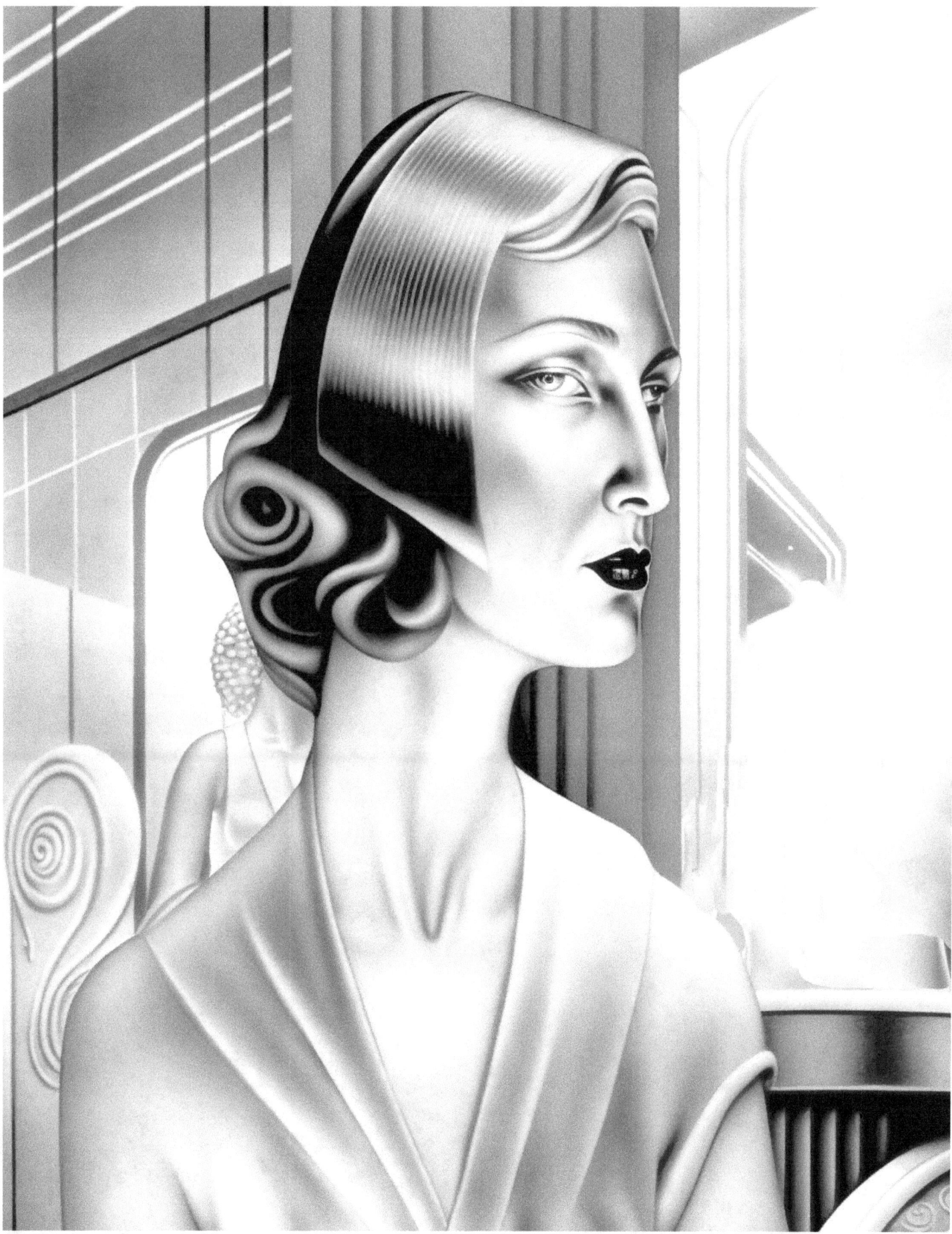

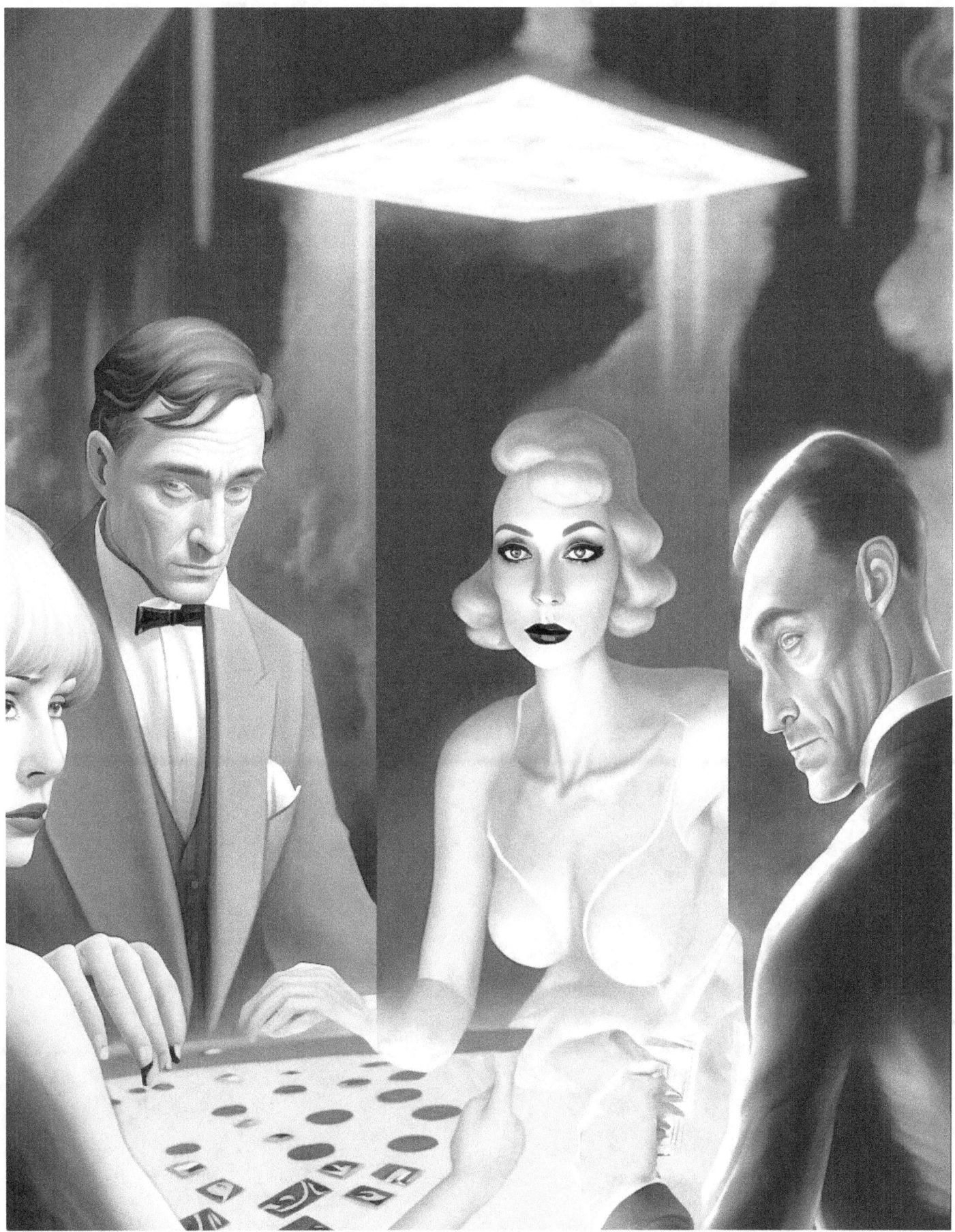

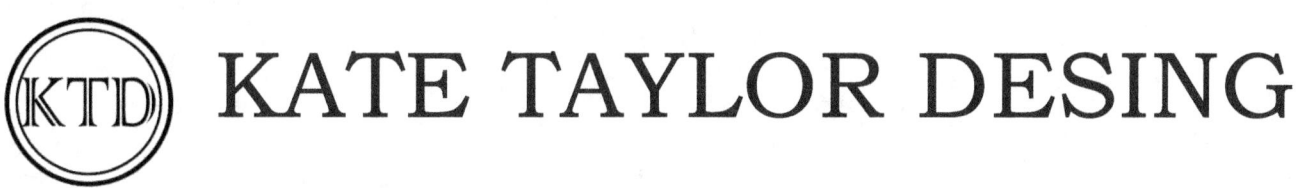

KATE TAYLOR DESING

OTHER COLORING BOOKS:

MYSTICAL CREATURES

- A Dragon Coloring Book for Adults
- A Unicorn Coloring Book for Adults
- A Phoenix Coloring Book fo Adults
- A Fairy Coloring Book for Adults
- A Mermaid Coloring Book for Adults
- A Goblin Coloring Book for Adults
- A Gnome Coloring Book for Adults
- A Troll Coloring Book for Adults
- A Gryphon Coloring Book for Adults

VEHICLES

- American muscle cars coloring book for kids
- Supercars coloring book for kids
- Antique car coloring book for kids
- Jumbo cars coloring book for kids
- Motorcycle Coloring book for kids

THE HORRORS OF COLOR

- The Dark Carnival: A Coloring Book for Adult

- The Haunted Mansion: A Coloring Book for Adults

- The Curse of the Mummy: A Coloring Book for Adults

- Nightmare Bugs: A Coloring Book for Adults

- Dark Witchcraft: A Coloring Book for Adults

- The Spectral World: A Coloring Book for Adults

- Cemetery Chronicles: A Coloring Book for Adults

- Sinister Forest: A Coloring Book for Adults

- Vampire Dreams: A Coloring Book for Adults

- Horror coloring book

MANDALAS AND PATTERNS

- Geometric shapes and patterns coloring book

- Adult coloring book tessellations patterns

- Adult coloring book geometric patterns

- Adult coloring book circular patterns.

- 150 Mandala coloring book

ARTISTIC ADVENTURES

- Surreal Escapes: A Coloring Book for Adults
- Cubist Explorations: A Coloring Book for Adults
- Impressionist Sensations: A Coloring Book for Adults
- Art Nouveau Revival: A Coloring Book for Adults
- Art Deco Magic: A Coloring Book for Adults

QUOTES

- Inspirational quotes from the bible coloring book
- Money quotes coloring book
- Quotes for success coloring book
- Funny Mom Quotes and Patterns coloring book
- Motivational swear words coloring book

CHILDREN

- The Toddler Coloring Book
- Unicorn Coloring Book
- Dinosaur Coloring Book
- Mermaid Coloring Book
- Kawaii Friends Coloring Book